THE THREE GODS
OF INCARCERATION

THE THREE GODS OF INCARCERATION

KIM HARMON

Author's Note: To say that I have learned the principles in this book, through the study of God's Word, would be a drastic understatement. In studying many translations of the Bible, however, I often use "layman's terms" in expressing scriptural quotes, in order to make the meaning as clear and accurate as possible. Sometimes the terms are even baser than this, almost "street" terminology, because this is where the giants live. Since the translations we are reading might differ slightly, you will seldom find a "word for word" quote in this manuscript. What you will find is that I am thoroughly committed to the Bible, to its power, to its accuracy, and to its consistency.

Scripture quotations marked (NIV) are taken from the Holy Bible, New International Version ®. Copyright © 1973, 1978, 1984 by International Bible Society Used by permission of Zondervan Publishing House. All rights reserved.

Scripture quotations marked (AMP) taken from the Amplified® Bible, Copyright © 1954, 1958, 1962, 1964, 1965, 1987 by The Lockman Foundation. Used by permission." (www.Lockman.org)

Printed in the United States of America

Publishing services by Selah Publishing Group, LLC, Tennessee. The views expressed or implied in this work do not necessarily reflect those of Selah Publishing Group.

ISBN: 978-1-58930-240-2
Library of Congress Control Number: 2009910879

- Dedication -

This book is to the giants.
They have been asleep,
but I pray they hear the trumpet blast,
that they arise,

that they understand, once and for all,
that their journey was never meaningless,
that their insignificance was only temporal,
that their weakness,
coupled with the power of God,
will turn the earth upside down.

Giants come in many forms; There are giant sales,
giant tasks, giant debts.

No giant will ever be as revolutionary,
as unexpected, or as explosive,
as the one to whom
this message is addressed.

This giant will never die,
it will never be defeated,
it will laugh,
and produce light to guide home
all those who choose to be their children.

To Jesus Christ,
to my husband, one of the giants, and
to my children, uniquely called to lead them.

CONTENTS

Section 6 - Who God Is

Section 7 - Stomping Their Feet

Introduction

SLEEPING GIANTS

This prophecy was given to me regarding four groups of people, (1) the incarcerated, (2) the addicted, (3) the homeless, and (4) the mentally ill. At the end of the prophecy, the Lord referred to them as, *"the hidden, the rejected, the wandering and restless, outcasts, prisoners & addicts."* He *seemed to be saying that their real titles were, "the Warriors, the Passionate, Seers, Hearers, Listeners, Watchers and Feelers."* I saw them, and wept, as He spoke:

"Because you feel what I feel, and you see what I see, I am using you in unusual ways. I have chosen you to <u>unveil the treasures</u> that have been hidden, and put away by man."

"There will be a battle, but you must not give up or give in. You must be convinced that these are not just your ideas, but ideas born in the heart of your Father."

"I have chosen you, 'for such a time as this,' because the battle to come will be such that the army that exists (in the church) today will not be sufficient to withstand the numerous attacks."

"The attacks on my people will be both subtle and terrible. The new 'division' of My army can see it coming, but they need healing and encouragement in order to step into the heat of the battle. The healing will come through Truth, Truth that you will carry to them."

"This part of My army has been <u>hidden</u> in hospitals and under highways. They've been <u>suppressed</u> by negative words and medications. They have been <u>diverted</u>, but only because I allowed it. For a time, I let Satan deceive them, and even hide them from My own people. Like a spiritual Navy seal team, or troops of Green Berets, they are <u>special forces</u> who will surprise and overwhelm the enemy."

"I will send people to you, who will receive this word, and fight beside you. You will know who they are. They will be trustworthy and willing to make the sacrifices required, losing reputation, losing self, willingly entering the battle because <u>they are convinced</u> that this is the word of the Lord. You must also be convinced. The battle will be heavy, but I will lead you," says the Lord.

Over and over, within just a few days, this prophecy was confirmed to me. I believe that God is saying that my job is to tell these people who they are.

It was December, 2005. The night it came, I felt the adrenalin rush through me, and panic seized me. It felt as if the words He'd spoken had never been uttered, not in all of time. Like some monumental archeological dig, unearthed for the first time, the words astonished me. They were real, and they would impact my life as none others ever before, nor since.

The next four years of my life I watched and listened to those around me. I'd already spent six years working with the homeless, those battling addiction and people caught in the revolving doors of the prison system. But now I had new information. As if I'd always known, those six years had been filled with uncertainty; was I helping them, or were they somehow destined to help me? With the declaration of God now in my spirit, uncertainty was replaced with understanding. Yet what I understood was not common knowledge, and often attracted controversy among members of mainstream society. Even Christians had been reluctant to acknowledge that the people they had patronized and "reached out" to were, in fact, those who would one day lead them. Most of all, those caught in cycles of obsession and sin had been convinced they were second-class citizens for generations. God knew who they were, and surely had convinced me, but how would I convince them?

One day in 2007, just before a horrible tragedy that left me emotionally bankrupt and without a job, God told me he was "freeing my hands." I'd always wanted time to spend on writing and worship (I'm a musician) and in this moment it felt as if He was making a promise.

Less than a month later, what seemed the most painful moment of my life occurred, and I was to discover what Romans 8:28 **really** meant, that when God said "all" things would work out for good for those of us who love and serve Him, He meant, "amazing wonders from bloody devastations."

Eighteen months of healing time passed, and enough tear shedding to warrant buying flood insurance. God never left my side, and now He would speak again. I'd spent many hours in solitude with Him. Even my family and friends backed off, as they saw the tremendous work God was doing. But what they didn't see was the continuous and powerful download of His Word, confirming that prophecy He'd given me two years before. Pages and pages of handwritten notes, some written on church bulletins, others on napkins taken from restaurant counters, made their way to typed pages, and then to this book. This time, He said,

"Tell them what you've learned."

I pray the pages you read will show you that you are part of an army. Though it has been asleep, the Spirit of Truth has begun to shake it. Why now? Because you are needed, and we haven't much time.

SECTION ONE

The Feast of the Gods:
Anger, Lust & Fear Exposed

*"The cowering prisoners will soon be
SET FREE;
they will not die in their dungeon,
nor will they lack bread."*
Isaiah 51:14 (NIV)

Chapter One

THE FEAST OF THE GODS
- WHO THEY ARE -

"You shall have no other gods besides Me...."
Exodus 20:3 (AMP)

Why are they considered gods? Anger? Fear? Lust? I **know** they're wrong, evil, damaging. But gods?

Anger: A feeling of displeasure resulting from injury, mistreatment, opposition, etc., and usually showing itself in a desire to fight back at the supposed cause of this feeling.

Lust: A **desire** to gratify the senses, as in seeking unrestrained gratification, sexual **desire**, overmastering desire (lust for power) intense enthusiasm, zest, inclination, to feel an intense **desire**.

Fear: A feeling of anxiety or agitation caused by the presence or nearness of danger, evil or pain. Timidity, dread, terror, fright, apprehension, unease, doubt, alarm, panic, worry.

Note: For the purpose of this study, **Lust** will be defined as <u>unhealthy **desire** for gratification.</u>

Principalities, strongholds, sins; whatever their names, they must simply be called on the carpet, exposed, acknowledged and dealt with! But when you name them anything as insipid as, "flaws," "mistakes," or "habits," you're simply assisting them in their conspiracy to remain inconspicuous. Remember, your worst enemies are always those you think of as harmless, or even friends. But these are not our friends, and the sooner we come to grips with that fact, the better.

Let's say, for example, that you lived in ancient Bible times. A new king comes to the throne in Israel, only to find the kingdom in tatters. He sets out to make improvements. Like our modern-day leaders, this man's political platform was based on making the world a better place. His campaign manager, had he needed one, would have worked hard to portray him as a caring, unselfish servant, who's only motive was to create a nicer place for people to raise their children. Of course, kings didn't have to run for office, or be elected, yet we see that many of them had slogans to sell, perhaps to gain popularity and thus more cooperation in maintaining order. Whatever the reason, kings back then tried to walk both sides of the fence, just as "they" do today.

Now, all of Israel's kings knew there was only one God. Even though the people they ruled were often sampling the cultures and religions of their neighboring countries, most of the kings made their own beliefs clear. There are many instances in which they are seen consulting prophets and seers in order to find <u>Jehovah's</u> will or plan. But kings back then weren't much different than our leaders today, and few of them every truly confronted Israel on the **real problem**, even though the true prophets of God spelled it out for them again and again. All through the books of History and the Prophets, we read that Israel, **"...served other gods...."** (Deut 29:26 - Josh 24:2 - Jud 2:12- Jer 5:19) So, why didn't the kings make a deal out of it? Why didn't they make proclamations condemning Israel's whorish behavior? Well, they did.

The kings of Israel and Judah, for the most part, publicly condemned the two-timing practices of the Israelites, and so, appeared quite righteous. But most of them never **acted** on their beliefs. Like tired traffic cops, these kings not only tolerated violations, but even went as far as to entertain

various leaders of these heathen nations, offering them aide, refuge, and military collaboration.
Still, nothing was ever said about **the problem**.
Further evidence that these kings were people-
pleasing pansies was in the fact that only a hand-
ful of them ever removed the altars, temples and
"high places" of idolatrous worship that were right
there in Israel! In our modern society we would
say, "Well, those places have historical value," and
would have made museums or national parks out
of them! Back then, however, it was considered
more diplomatic to simply "leave **well enough**
alone," thereby keeping everybody happy; everyone except God, that is. Like us, these kings wanted to keep their friends, and not "make waves."
They paid dearly, however, often by having their
kingdoms ripped out of their hands. (I Kin 13: 33, 34;
II Kin 18: 3-7) Those who did, in fact, take action and
tear down those high places are among the most
successful of all the kings. (II Chron 11:15-17 and 12:5-9)

Most of them didn't make the connection, I
guess, but fortunately for us, it's historically docu-
mented, and the evidence clear.

Not only do we see the pattern of blessing
with obedience, but we have the fulfillment of the
prophets' words that we can read about and learn
from. I Corinthians 10:11 says these things were

written for examples for us. Phew! Isn't it a relief to know we don't have to learn everything the hard way?

Okay, so let's determine why they are called, "gods," these issues of anger, lust, and fear and why we don't accept them as abstract feelings, temptations and pitfalls. In examining what a false god is, we need to look at motivations and results, both ours and theirs. Let's see. A god is something you worship, right? It's considered holy, and something to fear and obey, kind of like our God. A god would give orders, have preferences and opinions, and generally be in charge of our decision making processes. So how could anger, lust and fear be that? They aren't **living beings** with wills, ideas, minds, thoughts and motivations; or are they?

Coming from yet another angle, if I have a god, my behavior will be motivated by how much value I place on that god. The results of my day, every day, will be measured against how well I performed for that god. If I did what my god said to do, and this was evidenced by a succession of actions that lined up with that god's plan, I have pleased my god. To sum it all up, a god has an agenda, and I show my respect for that god by cooperating with that agenda.

Let's take ANGER, for example. If, for the sake of argument, anger is not an abstract feeling, but instead is an actual entity with a will, plan and agenda, and if I serve this god, the following would take place:

1) **Anger will convey its ideas to me.**

2) **I will, if I serve this being, listen carefully to these ideas.**

3) **Because it is my god, I will agree with its ideas.**

4) **Now that I agree with Anger, I will then proceed to act on this agreement.**

So, what would that look like? In examining anger, we can include some of its other names: frustration, impatience, distrust, depression, defensiveness and rage. Ever experience any of these? Because of the people and situations in our past, we all do. We've all been betrayed, so we often assume negative things about new relationships. We've all been criticized or abused, so we take things the wrong way. We actually believe someone will betray us, even when they're completely innocent! (This happens commonly when a person reminds us of someone from our past.) We start rehearsing the old hurts and remembering "what happened last time." We sometimes go so far as to **act** on that old memory, even though what's happening now isn't meant to harm us at all!

"But," you argue, "when I have decided to forgive someone from my past, how can that affect me in the future? I've put it behind me, right? And what has that got to do with a false god?"

Let's look back at our definition of a god. A god is something that makes demands, and if it is my god, I cooperate with these demands. Anger, in our example, is something that tells us people are trying to harm us, and can't be trusted. It often accompanies this with evidence from previous bad experiences. We rehearse Anger's idea, contemplate his false evidence and seldom even question its accuracy. <u>When I agree without question, I am giving great respect</u>, and in this situation, I am giving great respect to anger. And I usually call it, "**my anger!**" Yes, now, I've called it **mine!** To continue with this hypothetical scenario, as I contemplate and agree with these suggestions, I begin to plan my actions, the ways I will keep the person or persons from "getting to me." I immediately erect a "wall" between me and the other people involved, an emotional distancing, preventing me from caring deeply about them. I change the original plan

I had to have a close relationship, deciding that the pain I **might** have to go through is not worth the risk. I will now do things differently.

A god is something you obey. It's something you bow to, doing everything it tells you to do. You adjust your life around your god, and for it, you will be extremely flexible and compliant. Even those of us who proclaim, "I am my own boss. I do what I want to do, and no one better get in my way," or, "No one tells me what to do," have fallen to anger. Depression, frustration or acting out often surface and take the lead, the "reins" of our lives. Funny thing about anger is that it tends to come in pretty meekly and usually under another name. We seldom recognize it for what it is. We think of it as justifiable and give it tremendous access into our world.

Let's check out an illustration. You walk into the home of someone you met a few days ago, while at the park. This guy seemed very "real" to you, like he had nothing to hide, and just plain cared. He was super friendly, but not pushy, so you felt pretty relaxed around him. He even talked about God, like he wasn't embarrassed. You need a Christian friend, so you agreed to go visit.

You walk into his house, and the first thing you notice is that it's really a mess. Not like just things out of place, but there's trash on the coffee table in the living room, and you can see the garbage overflowing out of a wastebasket in the kitchen. It's a little gross, but no big deal, you decide. The guy's just not "anal." Since he yelled, "Come in," you figure he's just kind of a "kick back" person. He still hasn't come in the living room, where you're waiting, so you start looking around on the bookshelf. Then you see a picture of someone you recognize. It's a girl that you know really well, who you hang out with quite a bit, and she's in this picture with the guy you're visiting; she's hanging all over him! This is starting to feel weird, because you'd never seen this guy until a few days ago, but here he is in this picture with your friend. You start getting suspicious, wondering if there's some kind of "set up" going on.

"Hey, glad you made it!" He comes out, grinning from ear to ear, starts to give you a brotherly hug. You dodge it, though, just giving him the ole' "shoulder bump," because you're still thinking about the picture. You try to act cool, just listening as he tells you why he couldn't come to the door. He invites you to have a seat. You do, and then you find yourself looking at the picture across the room again. He sees you looking at it, and says, "That girl, wow! I was like, minding my own business and she hit on me, big time. I didn't even like her, but she was like really intense, and we ended up together. I don't know though, she's like, whoa, way like desperate or something." He laughs, like he's mocking the girl you are friends with. Now you're starting to feel the blood coming up your neck.

"No way, Dude. She's cool. I know her." You know he didn't say anything that bad, but you just can't help sticking up for the girl. She's always seemed really sweet; not cheap or "easy."

"Whatever, man." He drops it. "Hey, wanna go shoot some pool?"

You can't drop it. The guys a jerk, right? He might even be taking advantage of your friend. You don't think it's a set up anymore, but that got you edgy in the first place, and then he starts saying this stuff. You feel like you need to deal with it, to stand by your friend.

"Man, no way. You're on some other planet. Later." You start to walk away.

The guy just looks at you like you're totally crazy. "What's your problem?" he asks.

You've had it. You were about to walk out the door, but now you're really ticked. First he says stuff about your good friend, and now he's disrespecting you. You turn back toward him, take one step and let it fly. He goes sailing across the living room, landing on the sofa, and just lays there. You leave.

First, in the example, you were looking for a friend. The guy seemed nice, and you needed that in your life. You were pretty sure he was a Christian, too, and thought maybe God made you cross paths with him. After you go in his house, tho', the mess kind of puts you off. You're not the cleanest, either, but you take out the trash before it overflows all over the place. The reason it grosses you out, though, is because you're younger brother used to trash your room all the time, when you were kids. You always ended up being the one to clean up. Not only that, but your brother used to take everything way too casually; he couldn't be serious about anything. People got hurt by that a lot, including you, so the whole "messy house" thing just didn't set very well.

Then you see your friend in the picture with the guy. Now she's someone you care about, and always acted really straight-laced and like she just wanted to be friends, with no romantic stuff. That was cool, even though you wouldn't have minded a little more. But then you see her with this guy you've never seen before, and its like, why him and not you? You get a little jealous. Plus, you're little brother had stolen a girlfriend or two in the past, and so this guy's reminding you of that, too.

When the guy says your friend is desperate, you basically want to kill him. First, she's not desperate, or why wouldn't she go out with you? Second, he said she was "intense," and that they ended up "together," meaning they slept together, right? You thought the guy was a Christian, and you also thought your friend wouldn't do something like that, so now you're feeling pretty much like you can't trust either one of them. You even had this weird thought, "I hate these people," while you and the guy were talking. So, you ended up hitting him.

Later, you see your friend, the one the guy had the picture of. You see her same smile, and she's just as friendly as always. You try to act casual. You ask her about the guy, and she says, "Oh yeah, I met him at a dance. No one would dance with him, so I kind of 'took a leap.' He looked lonely anyway, so I asked him to dance. It was fun, plus I think it made him feel more welcome."

Oh yeah, the dance! You hadn't gone, 'cause dances weren't really your thing, but there was a dance, AT THE CHURCH! The singles group had put it on, and now that you thought about it, your friend DID look kind of dressed up in the picture!

She continues, "Oh, and he was kidding with me about being desperate, too! I think he's kind of shy, so he wanted me to think he was confident or something. Anyway, I told him, 'Yeah, I really have a hard time getting boyfriends.' It was cool. Poor guy, he got a page from his work right after that, so he had to leave. How's he doing, anyway?"

Oh great! You feel like a total idiot. He was just joking about your friend being desperate. And he meant they DANCED together, not that they had sex! He probably thought your friend was really awesome. That's why he was laughing and joking about it! He likes her, like in a good way! But what really happened in that guy's living room?

Anger, the god of Anger was present. The reason you know that is because you REALLY overreacted, and misread what this guy was saying. Even though you thought God was in it in the first place, your old thoughts about your brother, and your protective thoughts about your friend came into play. The reason memories of your brother surfaced were because you never really dealt with it. You didn't even realize it, but you had never really forgiven him for some of that stuff. You thought it wasn't that big of a deal. Well, it didn't seem like a big deal now, but you remember that at the time, when your brother did the stuff, it really made you mad. That old "mad" feeling was still in you, and the god of Anger knew it! He set you up! He lied, telling you this guy was like your brother, a selfish slob taking advantage of a girl, a girl you were half interested in. Old wounds that had never healed got salt poured in them by this false god. It wasn't your normal self, it was something else, and something powerful that just "took over." Your thoughts and then your actions were all a result of lies!

We have reason to be angry about things that are unfair, cruel or simply wrong. When we see people getting hurt or mistreated, we and God get angry. But when something just gets all twisted, and the person we are seems to morph into some kind of monster we don't recognize, that is an entirely different issue. When that happens, it's because there is another source there with us, one that we've probably listened to many times before. That creature distorts what's REALLY GOING ON, and the results, like in our illustration, can be really serious, if not just plain embarrassing!

We need to learn the difference between normal anger, righteous anger, and anger that is initiated by an evil force. We need to know when we are serving something other than Jesus Christ. In the book of I John, scripture says that we need to keep ourselves from false idols. The Amplified Bible, taken from the original Greek text, and translated more clearly than most Bibles, clarifies what a false idol is: "...keep yourselves from idols (false gods) (from anything and everything that would occupy the place in your heart due to God, from any sort of substitute for Him that would take first place in your life). Amen (so let it be)."

When evil causes us to obey, serve or be influenced, we have allowed something to "substitute" for God's leadership, and the place of authority He has in our lives. We are now allowing a substitute dictator to take the throne of our hearts, instead of the Holy Spirit. That makes these "evils" gods, specifically, FALSE gods.

Always remember that if a god is something you agree with, obey and change your actions for, and if anger is well, **something you have agreed with, obeyed and changed your actions for,** anger can be more than just a feeling or emotion. The truth is, Anger, Lust and Fear are gods, so cowardly that they hide, denying their true identities. They are afraid, for they have been forced into lives of slavery. Their existence is only to agree with, obey and make <u>all</u> of their plans around <u>their</u> master, <u>their</u> god, their "king" of sordid kings!

Chapter Two

THE FEAST OF THE GODS
- HOW THEY FEED -
The Study of Strongholds

*"There is a way that seems right to a man,
but in the end it leads to death."*
Proverbs 14:12 (Mine)

Have you ever heard the word, "stronghold?" Basically, it means (according to Webster's Dictionary) "a place having strong defenses." Ironically, a second definition in this same resource says it like this, "a place where a group having certain views, attitudes, etc. is concentrated." Hmmm. Now, there are little add-ons to these definitions, referring to fortresses, or "fortified" places, that make this even more interesting, because the Bible tells us that strongholds are areas in our lives that need to be torn down! Further, in II Corinthians 10: 4 - 5, it describes the strongholds, "...arguments and every pretension that sets itself up against the knowledge of God, and we take captive **every** **thought** to make it obedient to Christ." So we know there are groups with certain views involved. We also know that it's a (relatively) "strong" group, thus the name, "stronghold." Third, we know that this group is arguing with God, and **intentionally** setting itself up against what God knows, i.e., **TRUTH!** Finally, the bad news is that this group's conference room is set up in, where? Our thoughts!

Well, the good news is, all that *@!*#! going on in your head wasn't **your** idea, but unfortunately, we can't escape all responsibility, as the passage clearly states that we're the ones who have to take those guys captive! So, the defense made so famous by comedian Flip Wilson, "The devil made me do it!" won't work for God. And since a stronghold is a group, or a fortified place, who is this group that's **fortifying** it? I am sooooooo glad you asked!

The Bible tells us who they are, that they are not "flesh and blood," but "...rulers, authorities, the powers of this dark world, and...spiritual forces of evil in the heavenly realms!" (Eph. 6: 12) That's not you, and that's not me! That's not anything human! Want more proof? It goes on to say in Ephesians 6 that the weapons we use against these guys are, "truth," "righteousness," "readiness (from the gospel of peace),""faith," "salvation," and "the sword of the Spirit, which is **the Word of God**!" (Eph 6:13-17) So the weapons are <u>not</u> the kind you use against people, not "carnal," (King James) or the "natural weapons of the world," but have "divine power." (II Cor 10: 4)

Okay, so now we've got something to work with. We've got some beings, not human beings, who argue with God. We've got the idea that they are somewhat strong, at least, influentially speaking. (Satan is described as a "roaring" lion, in I Peter 5:8, implying that he makes a sound, "roaring," that is intimidating.) So we know that the members of this group both speak and argue. We also know that they've set up camp in our heads, but how? Through the means of the spiritual world, they are able to communicate with us, and unfortunately, because we don't usually hear their voices audibly (although some of us do) we don't address them or correct their lies. Yes, lies. These entities are incapable of speaking truth (Jn 8: 44) because, as the Word says, their ideas exalt themselves against God's knowledge, God, who is Truth! (Jn 14: 6 - Jn 15: 26 - Jn 17: 17) Through our innate spiritual person, the part of us God built so we would see beyond the natural realm, these evil forces connive, influence, persuade and demand things of us. They are constantly formulating their views, or opinions, within the spirit realm. Even when we haven't had a chance to decide how **we** feel about a matter, they are quick to make their suggestions. Often, before we've had the opportunity to pray, to bring our questions and concerns to God, we've already fallen "prey" to the predictions of these rulers of darkness. The gods! We begin, again, to obey them, to bow to their every whim, and to serve their agendas, because we are often **completely unaware of them!**

Ultimately, the gods, Anger, Lust and Fear have the say so, until we say no. Let me say that another way. Until you **turn it** off, their accusations and persuasions will keep coming at you, like a sick tape recorder playing over and over in your head. This powerful, repetitive dialogue is a stronghold. Like being in a rut, we get stuck there, and after all, why should they come up with something new, when the old stuff seems to work just fine? They say things like, "That will never work," "You'll feel much better when you have that," and "These people are lying to you; they think you're stupid!" Funny thing is, we blame ourselves for these ideas, thinking they originated with us, but like Solomon said, "There's nothing new under the sun," (Eccl. 1: 9) and that includes the traps and tricks of Satan! The condoning of abortion might be new, but offering children up to the god or goddess of sexual "freedom" is one of the oldest sins on the planet! New name, same problem. How about racism? Read Song of Songs, and you'll find the object of Solomon's love is a dark woman ("dark and lovely") (Song of Songs 1: 5, 6) who was embarrassed about the color of her skin, considering it a disqualifier for receiving the king's affection. She was also discriminated against because she was a woman, but then, most people are aware of how far back THAT one goes!

Have you ever noticed that people who don't have a relationship with God think evil is an abstract thing that comes to tempt them, and they themselves are the good guy? They say it's their own "conscience" that helps them resist temptation. So the evil is abstract, and the good is them. Christians, on the other hand, aren't always much wiser! For the most part, if you ask a Christian to describe this process, they will tell you that <u>the evil is them</u> and the good is God! Yet, the very first, **precedent-setting** sin recorded in the Bible originated with Satan! Eve didn't come up with the idea to eat the forbidden fruit. **She just listened** to the argument against God's **knowledge**. (Gen 3: 1 - 6) Sound familiar? Is she innocent? No, but the issue here is not whether or not we're responsible for our own disobedience. That's the easy part, and as was mentioned, we're already real good at

taking the blame. The only part we keep missing is that we are being influenced. And pushed.
There are real beings, actual entities that we have
neglected to **identify and confront! And they
feed each other!** Anger, Lust and Fear are the
advisers recommending actions that result in sin.
Not only the Holy Spirit, but also evil spirits have
something to say about everything. They hide behind each other, and pass the buck too. Often,
when we fall into temptation, we hear the words,
"It was because I was angry," or, "It was because
I was afraid," or, "It was because I just wanted it
so badly!" They often blame each other. "I got
scared because he was angry," "I was depressed (a
form of anger, actually repressed anger) so I went
out and bought (desired) all these clothes!" Now,
we're in the blame game, we're in the Stronghold
Conference Room, and not saying a word. Everyone is pointing fingers now, and we just sit there,
confused. We allow it, because we don't recognize
who is talking. We think the thoughts originate
with us! The thoughts are ours for sure, but the
origin? Our passive position is the result of not
recognizing our enemy. But our assertive action,
knowing God's Word and using it will "set us free."
(Jn 8: 32) When we begin to understand "Truth," as
Jesus described, and use it as Paul explained, we
have in that understanding the authority to turn
off the tape recorder! "Shutting the mouth of the

lion," (Heb 11: 33, Dan 6: 22) really isn't so hard; we only need to declare God's Word, and speak it out. This is what the Bible means when it says, "Resist the devil, and he will flee from you!" (Jas 4: 7)

I once dealt with these gods more heavily than I do today. During a 17-year long dysfunctional marriage, these subtle gods began to rule me. I remember a particular example of this, when I had become aware that there was more going on than just the desires of my own evil sin nature. Now we have that, for sure, but sometimes you just **feel** there's more going on than meets the eye.

Many things began to connect for me, as the harder things got, the more I pressed into God. Funny how that works, and precious. The more I cried out, the more His Word took on meaning, and became a weapon. No longer could people convince me that His Word was a rule book that I was repeatedly failing to fulfill. I began to see that God had written me a love letter, a Father's instruction to His child, a child who would need advice and counsel for many battles and struggles.

It happened one morning when I was washing dishes and singing a worship song to myself (well, not to myself, to Jesus, but I mean, no other humans were listening). I was humming along, and suddenly, **from nowhere**, came this rush of adrenalin and anger. A thought (suggestion, idea, reminder) of something I'd been hurt by fluttered in right in the middle of my worshipping, and just doing an everyday chore! I became immediately enraged, and then, because of my exposure to so much truth, it dawned on me, "This isn't me!" I literally felt a presence in the room. Off to one side, behind me and to my left, I felt something there. I didn't turn around, but I could **feel it!** I said, "Anger, you are not my god! I used to do everything you told me to do, but <u>no</u> <u>more</u>! I used to bow and scrape and grovel, every time you showed up. But I serve Jesus Christ now, the God of forgiveness and love. You want me to be bitter, to be miserable, and to eventually say or do something foolish and hurtful. I refuse to cooperate with you anymore, so **leave right now, in the name of Jesus Christ!** It is He, and He alone that I serve!"

Nearly as suddenly as the anger came, it left. I was shaking, but not with bitterness. I was still angry all right, and began to weep, but I now knew my enemy was not flesh and blood. It wasn't the person who hurt me; someone who had been influenced just like I had. It wasn't even myself I was angry at, but the tears that spilled endlessly from me were tears of grieving over years of imprisonment, years of incarceration! If only I had known sooner what I'd come to know on this day. Yet, I was triumphant, too, because I knew that, even though battles would continue to come, and even though I would never look forward to them, I had my Father's letter, containing all the strategies of heaven. I could feel His gentle love, and even sensed His smile of relief: "She gets it! Hey, she gets it!" And I did. And I want you to get it too.

Chapter Three

THE FEAST OF THE GODS
- HOW THEY DOMINATE & CONTROL -
The Study of Condemnation

"As obedient children, do not conform to the evil
desires (lusts) you had when you lived in ignorance..
But...be holy"
I Peter 1: 14, 15 (Mine)

The word, "holy," means, "consecrated to God," and "untainted by evil." It comes from the word, "whole," meaning complete. When Jesus declared someone, "whole," He used the Greek word, "sozo," which meant, "wholeness in body, mind and spirit," thus the reason religious leaders were offended. Jesus was pronouncing people completed, or "perfect," and He as the one who could grant this! Who, but God, could make someone perfect?

When we are whole, or complete, there is nothing left to do, to acquire, or to fix. We often sigh, when we have finished a task, such as a math test, or an auto repair. This sigh, more like a "sigh-hum," marks the end of something unpleasant, and the pleasure that comes with it. We "sigh-hum" when we feel content, such as after talking something through or after a long crying spell. It is at this time that we have a momentary sense of fulfillment; we are in a state of serenity and peace. We feel whole.

Lust, or the unhealthy desire for personal gratification, is one of three "gods," (Anger, Fear and Lust) who will never grant us peace. Lust, specifically, has no demarcation or boundary. It is endless, and will never be satisfied. Peter wrote that we should pursue holiness (wholeness) not perishable things. (I Pet 1: 14 - 24) He had his own experience with lust. Being discontent and unsettled were evidence of an area in Peter's life in which he needed Jesus' "wholeness," (holiness) and peace. (Jn 13: 10) This lack of peace caused Peter to be somewhat impulsive, often acting or speaking before he thought things through. Seldom seeing his error until after the fact, he was an easy target for condemnation. Although conviction is a tool of the Holy Spirit, in which He warns us before we fall into sin, and by which He reminds us of our sin, He never uses it to condemn us. **Condemnation**, on the other hand, is the tool of the gods, <u>the language they use</u> to dig up things of the past for which we have already been forgiven. Unlike the

Holy Spirit, Who is appeased as soon as we confess and repent, these spirits are never satisfied. The dissatisfaction that they convey is that unsettled feeling we get when we rehearse past failures; they rehearse them, and we listen!

In Peter's experience, it appears that he was getting "stuck" in his failures, and Jesus gently and discreetly sent Him a message of peace. While Jesus was washing Peter's feet, Peter's insecurity came to the surface. "...Not just my feet, but my hands and my head as well!" Although masked as humility, it was really **condemnation** that prompted this response to Jesus' gracious act. Symbolizing His forgiveness, Jesus' act of foot washing was to call attention to His cleansing ability, not to the dirt on the disciples' feet! But Peter couldn't see past his own failures. When he blurted out his desire for more cleansing, Jesus instantly recognized that desire as out of balance. Knowing that no amount of reassurance would ever satisfy Peter's insecurity, Jesus wisely interrupted Peter's train of thought with an illustration. "...a person who has had a bath <u>needs only to wash his feet</u>; his whole body is (already) clean. And you are clean...." Knowing Peter would later deny Him, (Jn 13: 38) Jesus lovingly comforts him in regard to his current brokenness, and also prepares him for that future failure. Peter needed peace, and to know that when he later "got his feet dirty," Jesus would still consider him "clean;" Confession and repentance would be all that was needed to "wash his feet!" (After Jesus' resurrection, we see Peter back in full relationship with Jesus. Compare this with Judas, the betrayer of the Lord, who hung himself. **Condemnation** ended the relationship.)

These are examples of **condemnation**. Peter displays what so many of us feel, that continual sense of failure. This sense is an open door for the enemy, as it evolves into unhealthy desire for gratification, that is, lust. The pain of failure drives us to find a way to ease that pain, and Lust is always ready with suggestions. Instead of pointing us toward confession, forgiveness from God and cleansing, Lust reminds us of our failures, using the language of condemnation, then begins to propose numerous ways to escape our misery. Fear and anger are quick to join in; in the "conference room of the gods," the one set up in our heads, they argue that there is something other than Jesus that will solve our dilemma. Fear discusses hiding our guilt, Anger suggests revenge, and blaming someone else, and Lust, the most clever and deceptive of them all offers "comfort" through any number of means. They are partners, and their "partnership" consists of first reiterating our failures, and then suggesting ways to find "relief." Referred to as "negative self-talk," it is the language of condemnation that lust, fear and anger use to dominate and control us. We can accurately compare this sick team effort to the pharmaceutical company that creates a drug to relieve pain, fully knowing it is not a cure, and in fact will cause side affects that will require yet another drug. Instead of addressing the original cause of the pain, bringing repair to the ulcer, headaches or arthritic joints (like holistic treatments can do - notice the word "holy" in "holistic"!) the pharmaceutical company simply creates medicines to treat symptoms; this becomes an endless pursuit, thus guaranteeing the manufacturer future sales from **customers with unmet needs**. (The word "pharmaceutical" comes from the Greek word, "pharmakeia," meaning "witchcraft!" and "domination and control.") Imagine what would happen to their sales, if these companies spent all their finances <u>to look for cures</u>! This is an unrealistic notion, of course, yet it begs the point that neither those companies, nor the evil forces we are studying have our best interest at heart! They are merely counterfeiters, posing as sources of relief and comfort, but in actuality, gifted salesmen, selling us whatever they can to keep us hooked!

SECTION
TWO

Exposing Anger

Chapter Four

Exposing Anger
- Anger Manifests -

"Be angry, and sin not."
Ephesians 4:26 (Mine)

Anger has many names. Among them are:

Irritation	Annoyance
Frustration	Disgust
Impatience	Domination
Depression	Mental Accusation
Rage	Self Pity

He manifests in different ways:

Increased Volume	Gossip
Silence	Isolation
Abandonment	Suspicion

Intimidation	Ulcers
Sarcasm	Headaches
Violence	Fatigue
Ridicule	Disrespect
Revenge	Stalking
Addiction	Avoidance
Lust	Fear

No matter the label, or the way this god chooses to demonstrate its personality, in concise terms, it is one very disgusting thing. Although it will try to masquerade as anything else, when exposed, its true identity is revealed: **<u>unforgiveness</u>**.

Anger is a god who asks much of its servants. One of the most physical of the gods, it demands an aggressive stand on all matters.

This god is unconcerned where its energy is directed; it only wants death and destruction to be the result. Whether you, its subject, cause harm to others, or turn the energy inward, Anger's pleasure is found as life leaves; leaves you, leaves your relationships, leaves your faith. Anger is out to kill.

Now, this god has an extremely persuasive argument, and its greatest advocate in recent history has been our system of democracy, for this is the root of the "entitlement" mentality. "I want my rights," is anger's favorite theme.

Anger will also keep lists of wrongs for every one of its servants to rehearse. Acting as our eager office assistant, Anger's memory is phenomenal, packing ideas into both the conscious and subconscious realms of its victim's minds. This is one of its most useful strategies, for once lodged in the memory banks, these lists can be accessed over and over again. The usefulness of these lists never diminishes over time, but actually increases in the ability to influence the human vessel in which they dwell. Each time the list is brought up, it has the unique power to cause more pain than the time before. In most cases, these lists are attached to people's names. Anger cares nothing about which person is blamed, so loose, fuzzy memories are portrayed as concrete facts and figures. Even if Anger's human container is blaming him or her self, pain is being inflicted, therefore Anger is satisfied.

Now it is important to add that not all anger is sin, and certainly Ephesians 4:26 makes this clear, when it says, "Be angry...." It certainly doesn't have a double meaning here, but clearly validates true, righteous anger. If anger was wrong, we would never see God displaying anger, yet when we read the Word, this is a repeated event! Even Jesus, God's "human" container, was furious at times, and not only knocked over the merchants' tables set up in the temple, but repeatedly used sarcasm when he was being challenged by the Pharisees. You may not agree, but calling them, "Vipers," and "White-Washed Caskets, clean on the outside, but inside full of a dead man's bones," was, well, a pretty clear sign that He was mad. Anger is valid, and is literally, a "motivation to correct injustice." The god of Anger, however, twists these God-given emotions into weapons we use against ourselves, each other, and worst of all, our Lord!

Chapter Five

Exposing Anger
- Anger's Target -

"There are things the Lord hates, (and one is)
a man who stirs up dissension among brothers."
Proverbs 6: 16, 19 (NIV)

Committed Relationships Challenged

Anger's <u>chief</u> target, of course, is you, but this monster is particularly fond of mass destruction. The serial killer of the gods, Anger's desire is to cause division between God's children. As one of Satan's disciples, Anger was thrown out of heaven along with his master, and has had these thousands of years since to develop a hatred for God that we cannot fathom. This "god," who defies the true God, targets His children and their relationships, a form of "payback" to the Creator. Now his job would be much more difficult if the Lord did not love us so much, but since God is,

"...compassionate," and "...rich in love," (Psalm 103:8) anger is often successful at causing Him pain.

Once welcomed in the courts of heaven, the god of Anger is now among those eternally evicted. We, God's people, can experience forgiveness and be restored to our relationship with Father God; he, Anger, cannot. And yes, he is very angry!

Because we were created for the purpose of a two-way love relationship with God, we have been given the opportunity to be saved from the destruction of sin. This is why the "gods," Anger, Lust and Fear, insist on attacking us, endlessly, intently. They are already doomed, and have nothing to lose. Yet, if they can destroy us, dissuade us from loving God, they receive some sense of equality with us! Until then, we are superior. Since we are less supernaturally equipped than they are, our position above them is a real slap in the face! It would be like a race horse, faster, stronger, more disciplined, yet loaded with weights (called handicaps) losing a race to a slower, less capable horse!

Revenge is their ultimate glory, and those God loves are the perfect prey. Their method of operation is to "divide and conquer," separating us from each other, and ultimately from Him. Most people who fall to the spirit of Anger end up with virtually no family and no friends. The few who dare to stay in relationship with the angry person do so out of fear, or some desperate need to feel valuable. Eventually Anger almost always succeeds in destroying everyone involved.

Chapter Six

Exposing Anger
- Anger's Face -
Identifying the Enemy

Angry People look like the following:

The Aggressor

Behavior Issues: (toward people, authority, living creatures, inanimate objects, all relationships)

These people are demonstrative, even when anger is not being displayed. They can be extremely, even **overly** affectionate, and "extremeness" is a telltale sign, although not necessarily aggressiveness.

Inwardly, the "reactive" slaves of this spirit often have health issues such as arthritis, stomach ulcers, headaches, self-inflicted injuries (whether intentional, or due to being "accident prone.") Health issues become more problematic when obedience to Anger leads to drug and alcohol abuse, food abuse, or other means of self abuse.

The "Aggressor" is who we usually think of when we describe an angry person. He or she experiences a pressure build-up when under stress. This build up results in the need to "let off steam," and the person then "vents" by directing hostility at another person. Over time, it takes less and less stress to produce the blow ups, and the outbursts become more frequent. At this point, the Aggressor usually begins "self-medicating," in an attempt to minimize the aggressiveness, using things such as alcohol, cigarettes, vicodin, heroin, marijuana and "comfort" foods, among others.

THE ISOLATOR

Attitude Issues: (toward people, authority, living creatures, inanimate objects, all relationships)

Just as destructive in every sense of the word, the "Isolator" has health issues as well. He or she is more likely to direct his or her anger inwardly, and can even appear somewhat docile and harmless. This is the intent, as this person will hide their true feelings by any means possible. This is because the Isolator, as compared to the Aggressor, is more codependent, that is, more concerned about the opinions of others, and is more lacking in a clear sense of self. Generally, the choice to "keep secret" his or her anger results in sporadic explosiveness. For the most part, the explosions take place privately, thus, the person looks for places to isolate. Not only does this person desire to escape these feelings, he or she feels compelled to escape the reality of his or her true condition, and the watchful eyes of friends, family or anyone who might notice there is a problem. "Depression" is the socially acceptable persona of the Isolator, and usually the only sign this person allows others to see. **Depression, however, should never be mistaken for anything other than anger**. Because it is a repressed form of anger, it usually takes much longer for this person to admit there is a problem with anger and unforgiveness. Remember that unforgiveness is the true identity of anger. Most people who take on the personality of "depression" are in total denial that they are both mad and bitter, while the Aggressor willingly admits, even announces these facts!

The Isolator can be recognized by traits of avoidance, apathy, indifference, lethargy, lack of interest and submissiveness which are all considered passive-aggressive "red flags" because of the tendency to change dramatically when anger limits are reached.

Although both the Aggressor and the Isolator are capable of the **act** of isolating, the Aggressor will not stay there long, as opposed to the true Isolator, who favors being alone. When physical solitude is not an option, the Isolator finds comfort in keeping his views and opinions private, thus isolating his personality.

SECTION
THREE

Exposing Lust

Chapter Seven

EXPOSING LUST
- LUST MANIFESTS -

"But godliness with contentment is great gain."
I Timothy 6:6 (NIV)

Lust pretends to be many things. Some are:

Hunger	Success	Love
Motivation	Passion	Materialism
Tenacity	Fulfillment	Drive
Addiction	Affection	OCD*

*OCD: Common acronym of Obsessive-Compulsive Disorder

She manifests in different ways:

Emptiness	Exclusivity	Racism
Loneliness	Neediness	Codependency

| Anger | Fear | Peer Pressure |
| Manipulation | Workaholism | Corrupt Strategies |

Lust has the unique quality of making one feel a constant sense of need or "emptiness," as described on our list. This extremely crafty god is the most subtle and underhanded of the three. Her personality most resembles the con artist, appearing to be a well-meaning, thoughtfully-motivated creature, always promising fulfillment. Her nature is more similar to a mothering-type nurturer than the other gods, thus the reason she is referred to in the feminine.

Jesus spoke with a woman who was unknowingly serving the god of Lust. (Jn 4: 4 - 42) As the story goes, while Jesus sat resting at a well outside the city gates of Samaria, with no means to draw from it, a woman appeared, apparently to get water for her household. During the course of a lively conversation between the two, it was discovered that the woman had spent her life "searching." Yes, she was experiencing the emptiness that each of us knows all too well.

First, Jesus asks the woman for a drink. Knowing the "waves" He would create, since He was a "Jew," and Jews did not ordinarily speak with Samaritans, this story becomes nearly humorous as Jesus adeptly leads the woman into a conversation that will ultimately change her life! He instantly creates in her a sense of value, for He has "crossed boundaries" by talking to her in the first place! Seeing inside her soul, He cleverly uses something He knows she can relate to; her need for water. He tenderly adjusts the practical aspects of seeking, drawing and transporting a bucket of water, to the much deeper truth of the quest we all share for fulfillment.

As is common for many trapped in the web of Lust, the Samaritan woman had become involved in numerous unhealthy relationships. Whether it was she who had the most "issues," or any of her many ex-husbands, Jesus wanted to point her to the source of gratification that would end her search, once and for all. He knew He was that source!

Lust does not care where you go in your search. She is not on a mission for personal attention, and actually prefers to stay "under the radar." This god is quite clear that, once recognized, her power to influence will be instantly nullified. Therefore, she acts more as an usher, or hostess, guiding you in a direction, <u>any</u> <u>direction</u>, in your pursuit of peace and a sense of self worth.

As far as Lust is concerned, if she is able to convince her attendants (that would be us) that she is doing them a favor, assisting them in meeting some kind of "need," she will succeed in keeping us captive, and away from Christ. She points us toward any substitute, any thing she can find to replace Jesus' role as Life Giver. In our story of the woman at the well, Jesus told the woman (paraphrased) "If you knew to Whom you were speaking, <u>You'd be asking Me for a drink</u>; I have water that would satisfy your thirst FOREVER; I AM that water!"

Lust, therefore, in her willingness to try anything, has many, many expressions. From sugar addiction to sexual perversion, she is capable of going completely unnoticed. One common deception she uses, for instance, is to persuade us that we need attention. She will usually cause us to feel that we have become invisible, unnoticed, or unappreciated. She comes armed with a list of our personal attributes and abilities, and plays this recording over and over for us. Not only does she repeat the list, but makes it clear that no one else is aware of how important we really are! Thus, pride inserts itself through the door of lust, and we become narcissistic and egocentric.

In order to avoid any misunderstandings, and along the lines of our last few examples, it's important to realize that sexual lust is only one form of Lust. In the English language, and specifically in the language of the American church, the word "lust" usually paints a mental picture of infidelity and inappropriate sexual habits or behaviors. But that only reflects one area of which we have become aware. Lust has become "undressed" as it were, in her attempts to drag the body of Christ into sexual addictions. But unfortunately she remains in "stealth mode" in most of her other manifestations. Many of these other methods of operation are introductory phases that lead to other addictions, including those that are sexual in nature. Simple things such as peer pressure might initially cause a child to seek certain clothing or to use certain mannerisms, in order to fit in. These tendencies, when extreme, can be alerting us to "red flags," indicating the possibility that Lust has already begun her assault in the early stages of a child's development.

Lust, in her truest form, is absolutely insatiable. She is a seeker, and is the perversion of personality traits gone wrong. Foregoing the appropriate expressions, those of passion and seeking truth, lust instead avoids truth and twists passion. She leads us to every kind of distraction, often using entertainment as a means of comfort. She entices us to overindulge in these "comforts," such as gambling, smoking, eating, talking, competing, sex, work, socializing, nurturing, medicating, bathing and aggression. Some of her more subtle forms disguise themselves as leadership, helpfulness, integrity, destiny, spirituality, neatness and preparedness. These, of course, are considered good traits to have, yet when merely counterfeits of the real thing, will tend to distract us from a close, personal relationship with the Lord.

All in all, Lust teaches us that what we do and pursue will make us happy. God's Word teaches us that it is what we are and believe that lead to ultimate and lasting joy. When our actions or acquisitions take the place of our position in God, they are now preventing us from ever finding lasting contentment. As we try to "gain," we find ourselves, not on a path, but on an endless journey; we move, yet never get anywhere. It tires us, but doesn't build our strength and it makes demands of us, but never seems pleased with our efforts. Lust will never be satisfied, and yet we bow to her ideas and obey her every suggestion.

Chapter Eight

EXPOSING LUST
- LUST'S TARGET -

*"Set your affection on things above,
not on things on the earth."*
Colossians 3:2 (Mine)

INTIMACY WITH GOD AT RISK

In chapter 5 we learned that we are created for a distinct purpose, to have a love relationship with our Creator. As expressed by the old adage, "Necessity: the Mother of Invention," human scientists often create in order to make improvements. God did not need any improvements. In contrast to the "need" factor, it was God's huge heart that was the motivation behind His creation of mankind. Once created, we were the ones in need. God clearly demonstrated His understanding of this need in

His decision to create a "helpmate" for Adam, (-Gen 2:18) His compassionate intervention illustrated the value He places on relationship.

There is no doubt that He considers the absence of relationship undesirable.

Lust is in competition. She, as stated before, has no desire to be detected, or to receive credit for her efforts. Her mission is clear and frightening as she attempts to stop all those in the human "race," the race in which God is the prize waiting at the finish line. She is a master of disguise and substitution, and an expert liar. There are no lines she will not cross, no sense of right or wrong. <u>All that she craves is that God be alone</u>. Even a Christian can become her victim, if she can cause that believer to keep God at an arm's length, giving Him only partial access to their lives, but never closeness and trust.

Lust uses legalism to paint God as a harsh, unsympathetic ruler. She uses a sense of emptiness to preach that God is insensitive to our needs. She is horrified by only one thing, and will do everything in her power to prevent it. She fears most, that we will find a place in our Daddy's lap, a place where we are accepted in our brokenness, praised for our smallest efforts, and welcomed at all times. If ever we "taste and see that the Lord is good," (Ps 34:8) her influence over us is a thing of the past, and she knows it. Even though she is incapable of swaying a Christian's intellect, causing him or her to believe that God is distant and uncaring, Lust makes it her purpose to distract us from **experiencing** His tenderness. Coming to us as one who is concerned about our needs, in actuality she is doing all she can to create a huge chasm between us and the only One who can ever fill those needs.

In counseling, I am always astounded at how many people have never had the experience of God's total affirmation, comfort and desire for them. To illustrate this side of Him, I have told numerous clients that He really is that big executive in the sky, just as they've always believed, but that He is also a fanatical Father. I describe a scenario in which God is in an important "conference" with world leaders. Right at a crucial point in the meeting, there comes a knock at the door, interrupting the session. It is you, God's little child.

"Excuse me," God says, pushing away from the enormous table, where he sits as Chairman. "My child needs me. This meeting will have to be adjourned."

Still in mid-sentence, He laughs at the noise of your small feet racing toward Him, and at the "kerplunk" on His lap that knocks Him unceremoniously back into His chair! Your arms wrap trustingly around His neck, and the angels nod, smiling. World leaders exit the room, unsurprised that a small person whose name they do not know was able to take God's attention so easily. After all, they are there to meet with God as well, about matters of human importance. What could be more appropriate than for God to validate His own child's need for Him right at that very moment?

Lust is demolished by this scene. Her goal is to prevent anyone's knowledge that such a thing is possible. She will attempt to shoe you away. Like the disciples, who told several children that Jesus was too busy to be bothered, she will try to convince you that you are merely an interruption to more important matters. But Jesus will always, always say, "Let my babies come to me, and forbid them not. They are what My kingdom is all about!" (Matt 19: 14)

Chapter Nine

Exposing Lust

- Lust's Face -
Identifying the Enemy

Lust demonstrates herself through people in the following ways:

The Leech

Although a very unsavory picture comes to mind when the term "leech" is used, the characteristics of this little creature parallel almost exactly the personality of a person stuck in a world of self-absorption.

The dictionary defines a leech as this: (1) a worm that sucks blood or eats flesh, and (2) somebody who clings to or exploits somebody else, for self-serving purposes.

This person is most commonly described as "very needy." You will find this person's messages on your answering machine more often than those of your other friends. They will accost you in parking lots, often not giving you time to extract yourself from your car before starting a conversation. They will hold you "captive" to them, chattering endlessly, oblivious to anything around them, such as the fact that you're standing in the middle of the aisle in the produce department! Although this person will almost always be described as "unusually friendly," the use of the word "friendly" can be misleading. They **are** frequently wearing a smile as they approach, but this "open" appearance can quickly give way to disappointment, hurt and even anger, if their attempts to get your attention fail.

More often than not, a person with lust issues approaches those that he or she deems important, necessary and/or authoritative. They are insensitive to the needs of those they seek out, focused only on their own desire for acceptance and validation. This person, once shunned, is the proverbial "two face," leaping quickly from expressing their undying loyalty toward you to hurling slanderous accusations against you! Quick to gossip, to stir up discord, and to develop plots of revenge, the leech has not found his or her sense of esteem. In spite of a life spent trying to "fit in," this horribly deceived person is one of the loneliest people on the planet.

The Manipulator

Similar in some ways to the leech, the manipulator is very self-focused. This focus, however, can be fulfilled in a variety of ways, unlike the leech, who merely seeks attention.

The manipulator has been pointed toward the path of achievement. He or she looks for ways to attain, and these acquisitions come in many forms. Money, Sex and Power are among the most common things sought for by the manipulative person. Often stepping over the unfortunate, the less aggressive, or the naïve, a manipulator is often mistaken as a leader. If leading is a goal that this person succeeds at attaining, the results can be catastrophic. In most cases, a certain degree of leadership is at least perceived by this person, even if only as a parent or a representative of some common cause. Sadly, especially in the case of a parent, relationships with the manipulator are very damaging. In most situations, children of manipulators are forced to do one of two things: leave all personal desires and expressions behind, in an effort to keep the manipulator "happy," or to become even more proficient at the art of manipulation than the parent, thereby overpowering his or her predecessor.

Manipulators are connivers, cheaters, and liars. They will do whatever is needed to get whatever is desired. If they want money, they might work for it, but they are just as likely to embezzle it, or to cheat on their taxes. If they desire sexual gratification, they will try desperately to patronize the person whose cooperation is required. When power is what they seek, they're lives take on an aggressive, pushy and demanding approach. These power seekers are those we would describe as both demeaning and cruel. The god of Lust is both of these, and she drives us to aggressive, addictive behaviors, promising that final sense of satisfaction and accomplishment. But she is lying!

SECTION
FOUR

Exposing Fear

Chapter Ten

Exposing Fear
- Fear Manifests -

"There is no fear in love,
but love expels every trace of terror.
I John 4:18 (AMP)

Fear masquerades under many aliases. He has far more names than can be listed here, but these are a few of them:

Wisdom	Lethargy	Dread
Moderation	Structure	Cautiousness
Control	Pride	Procrastination
Atheism	Suspicion	Organization
Inflexibility	Terror	

He uses many tactics to manifest:

Worry	Anxiety	Impulsiveness
Uncertainty	Addiction	Hesitation

Vacillation	Panic	Skepticism
PTSD*	Lust	Anger
Confusion	Paranoia	Indecisiveness
Insecurity	Delusions	

*PTSD: Common acronym of Post-Traumatic Stress Disorder

Just like the other gods, the god of **Fear** has a healthy counterpart. As opposite as night and day, however, healthy fear and the fear brought on by evil have virtually <u>nothing</u> in common. We have been led to believe that they are similar, that it's difficult to distinguish one from the other. Determining the source of fear, whether it is the truth of God or the deception of Satan, is the key to understanding their differences.

Healthy fear carries with it a solid pillar of truth. Somewhere in its makeup, you will always find a clear, concise reason for its existence. Although it can come unexpectedly, it is less like confusion, and more like a "sense" or "feeling" that plans or ideas should be reconsidered. For the person who has practiced submitting to the voice of God, it is accompanied by a positive feeling, even thankfulness. Jesus said, in fact, that His "sheep," referring to <u>mature</u> believers (as opposed to "lambs") know His voice, meaning that **those who had heard His voice numerous times** had now begun to recognize it. (Jn 10: 4) When the Holy Spirit speaks in this manner, the person listening will experience a sense of relief, that the "hesitation" they are feeling will somehow protect them or prevent a crisis. The Bible further describes it as "**peace**." (Col 3: 15) A new Christian (one of the "lambs") might feel frustration, not having a track record to help him recognize this as the voice of God. This is easily countered, however, by a **willingness to pause, and to pray**. Flexibility is the key, as God is always faithful (Jas 1: 5) to produce more signs of His direction. Usually, the one who pays attention and obeys this sensation will see the numerous calamities from which they've been spared, creating a sense of security. Recognizing the voice of the Spirit gets easier with each situation, and the "close calls" we avoid time after time soon add up to clear evidences that we really are hearing from God!

The voice of the Spirit differs from the evil god of Fear, whose familiar theme song nearly always begins and ends with **questions**. The questions vary, but the common thread is their open-endedness. Instead of a single, concrete truth, **confusion** is the earmark of the god of Fear. The ideas brought on by the god of Fear are numerous, and quite often create circular thinking. Often he is not even starting the process, but merely waiting for cues from us that there is a decision to be made. Once He determines this is happening, he jumps into the process, constructing **a "vicious cycle" of**

conflicting ideas, usually "alternatives" to what we originally planned. Whether we are making a business decision, evaluating a relationship, or choosing what clothes to wear, Fear just looks for opportunities to imply that we will probably make a mistake. Anxiety follows, and the only thing clear is a sense of chaos! The situation seems impossible and solutions appear unattainable. **It is in this stage that God is portrayed as uncaring and uninvolved**. This voice is ugly, and Fear, trying to come across as Wisdom, is unable to duplicate the strong, secure experience of the counsel of God. Finally, **we begin to feel ignorant and undeserving of any help**, another sign that we are being manipulated by Fear. It is also the method he uses to steer us toward condemnation.

As said previously, condemning us is a tactic of the gods, to dominate and control their victims. This goal is clearly Fear's focal point, and he has used it to cause devastating behaviors like self-mutilation, suicide attempts, and what has been labeled as OCD. (***OCD: Common acronym of Obsessive-Compulsive Disorder**) These are only a few of the serious issues that stem from the partnership of the gods, Anger, Lust and Fear. Fear takes the prize, though, as the primary "voice" that they speak through. Like an ambassador of evil, Fear steps forward as their representative, telling us we are incapable of success, that we have a history of failure, and that whatever we attempt will end in disaster. Finally, once we have acted on our decision, Fear totals our score to show us that we should have listened, that we didn't measure up, and the results of our efforts are, as usual, poor.

<u>We urgently need to understand that the god of Fear is afraid</u>. He is terrified, and we can see this by his stealth methods. Rather than coming out in the open, announcing his identity, he sneaks around "like a roaring lion." (- I Pet 5:8) This god is compared to such a majestic animal because of his method of prowling in the cover of night, and because the sounds and suggestions it makes seem to come out of nowhere, like the roaring of a lion. Yet, unlike its namesake, it does not honor the Creator, and its instincts have been distorted. Judgment has been pronounced on this evil idol, and the book of Revelation indicates he will be "thrown into the lake of burning sulfur," along with his supervisor, Satan. (Rev 19:20) You can be sure Satan heard it when Jesus told his disciples the following:

> *"I tell you, my friends, do not be afraid of those who kill the body and after that can do no more. But I will show you whom you should fear: Fear him who, after the killing of the body, has power to throw you into hell. Yes, I tell you, fear him."*
> LUKE 12: 4, 5

The book of Revelation (Rev 20:10) further clarifies who it is that has the power to throw us into hell. No, it's not Satan! The "Him" who is seated on "the Great White Throne" of judgment **is God**. He is seen pronouncing judgment after which the "devil," the "beast" and the "false prophet" are thrown into the "lake of burning sulfur."

Shortly after this (Rev 20:15) we read that anyone whose "name was not found written in the book of life," was also, "thrown into the lake of fire." This last is why we can agree with Solomon that "The fear of the Lord is the beginning of wisdom;" (Prov 9:10) <u>that</u> kind of fear is the most excellent example of healthy fear!

God demands first position in our lives, and has made no room for "gray areas." As we learn to turn our backs on these false gods, Anger, Lust and Fear, we are freed from slavery. We honor Him who made us, and one day we will triumphantly "wave goodbye" to our enemy, as he is hurled into his everlasting prison. We are no longer incarcerated, but Fear will never be free.

Chapter Eleven

EXPOSING FEAR
- FEAR'S TARGET -

"Behold, I have given you authority
and power... strength and ability over all the power
that the enemy possesses,
and nothing shall in any way harm you!"
Luke 10:19 (AMP)

CONSPIRACY AGAINST DESTINY

In comparing healthy fear to evil fear, let's examine the "fear of falling." Because of this fear, we avoid things like leaping from precipices, racing down steep stairways, or jumping off of high rises while flapping our arms! This **healthy** fear preserves life! Yet the god of Fear," that dark, ominous voice that tells us to avoid anything that appears slightly risky, actually results in preventing life! In this example, the person serving this spirit refuses to travel by air, avoids hiking in the mountains, and becomes shaky looking out the window of a two-story building. This demonstrates the opposite nature of these two kinds of fear. While one preserves, the other prevents. Here we can see the insidious nature of this god, to keep its victims in bondage. **If it succeeds, Fear will put a stop to our destiny**. (Jer 29: 11)

Every time we venture out, longing to discover new realms and hungering to touch the people around us with God's love, the god of Fear lurks close by. **His ultimate objective is to exchange the vision placed in us by the Holy Spirit, for an endless list of limitations.** This is why the "shield of faith" (Eph 6:16) becomes so important to us. "Faith," that comes, "by believing God's word," (Rom 10:17) renews our excitement and puts the power of God back in view. We remember that God has lovingly promised safety and provision to those who love and honor Him; we see a realm in which we can live life to the fullest. Yet, even knowing that "no weapon formed against us will prosper," (Is 54:17) and that He is with us "even to the end of the world," (Matt 28: 20) we will never find the amazing purpose planned for us, if we continue serving the god of Fear.

Chapter Twelve

Exposing Fear
- Fear's Face -
Identifying the Enemy

Fear is exposed in the following ways:

Trust No One

Probably one of the most common symptoms of a person dealing with this spirit is lack of trust. In counsel, I have found this **inability to trust** to be one of the most frequent causes of spiritual and social death. Since trust is a necessary part of a healthy relationship, something inside of us always seeks it out, no matter how many times we've been betrayed. In the most serious cases, when a person has retreated from relationships altogether, it is finally no longer desired or expected. Those who call themselves "atheists" (*Atheists: People claiming that they believe God is non-existent*) are sadly among this group. They may continue to have relationships with other people, but they have given up on God, convincing themselves after numerous heartbreaks, that He could not possibly exist.

A common expression we use refers to, "honor among thieves." This phrase has probably come about primarily because those who have found themselves entrenched in lives of crime find this trait of "honor" or "trustworthiness" lacking in those they have relied upon. For the most part it has been unreliable, abusive or neglectful family members or role models that have led these men and women to believe that trustworthiness is a thing of story tales. Seeing it displayed becomes so rare that they begin to doubt that trustworthiness, loyalty and honor really exist at all! Still seeking relationship, they adopt new "families," that is gang members, cronies, homies, fellow drug users (calling them "bruthuhs") and pimps. These new friends <u>seem</u> more believable, because many of the virtues of mainstream society are not sought or portrayed. Monogamy, purity, virginity, integrity, and the work ethic are among the assets that are often abandoned by these groups. This lack of pretense causes the normally untrusting person to feel a certain amount of hope, because they perceive these associates to be non-hypocritical, to be more "real."

CONTROL AND RESPONSIBILITY

Inflexibility, or **the perceived need** to control the how, when, where and with whom of ones day to day activities, is a tell-tale sign that a person is dominated by fear. This characteristic comes from the desire to avoid reoccurrences of traumatic events. Severely controlling people are not always seen as controlling, but rather are perceived to be driven, organized, perfectionistic and responsible. They are, in fact, able to carry massive amounts of responsibility. Nearly always communicating a willingness to take on more, they are privately bitter and angry, believing that more is "expected" of them. They are often mislabeled as "Type A personalities," "good managers," or "workaholics." Habitually these "control freaks" suffer from physical afflictions such as ulcers, headaches, arthritis and allergies, as their enormous and usually bottled up levels of stress cause physical "meltdowns." Relationships naturally suffer, as this person is seldom able to be flexible with anyone else's opinions or preferences. Although fear is the instigator, anger and lust are quick to jump on the bandwagon here. The result is a difficulty in determining the root cause of relationship breakdowns and physical symptoms. If the fear is not addressed, consequences as severe as nervous breakdowns, mental confusion, panic disorders, OCD, and PTSD can occur.

FAILURE TO PROGRESS

I have called this "failure to progress," but previously described it in the "<u>Conspiracy Against Destiny</u>" section. People who go this direction, in their flight from things and situations they believe to be risky, **have a difficult time finishing** tasks and goals. The fear they endure becomes a huge barrier to reaching any form of success. They often have education, but no degree; work experience but no licenses or certifications. If they are creative people, they have a tendency to start project after project, moving quickly from one idea to the next, but failing to complete them. Low self-esteem causes an unusual amount of negative self talk. They can be viewed as modest, open or humble, when they are in fact ashamed, insecure and self-doubting. In the attempt to cover their fear, these persons might make every effort to be friendly, vivacious and social, sometimes even confident, but inwardly they are suffering from a constant fear of failure.

EXCITEMENT AND DRAMA

One of the most misunderstood indications that someone is dealing with fear is the "drama" factor. The need for attention drives this person to "magnify" and "exaggerate." Their secret fear is that they are not valued. Believing the attention to be an indicator of their worth, or necessity, the "drama queen" (or king) will have a tendency to misrepresent themselves and their experiences. In an attempt to gain position or to feel needed and important, he or she unintentionally becomes, "the little boy who cried wolf." Their peers don't take long to realize that they are "blowing smoke" most of the time. This results in alienation, or even worse, in their taking on the role of class clown or comedian, because those with whom they socialize don't take anything they say or do seriously. A vicious cycle arises in which they struggle for peoples' attention, are progressively given less and less, and struggle all the more. The fear they have that they are unnecessary, or even burdensome, seems well-founded, and a battle with depression (anger) usually follows.

SECTION
FIVE

Who You Are

Chapter Thirteen

WHO YOU ARE
- THE TRUTH ABOUT GIANTS -

"Don't be misled...whatever is perfect comes from our Father, <u>our Dad</u>...and we out of all creation, became His prized possession!"
James 1: 16 - 18 (Mine)

There is one thing Satan and his legions are afraid of. They fear it more than hope, more than faith, more than love. They will do everything possible to prevent you from discovering it. That one thing is truth. Their world is based on deception; it is the foundation under their feet. They live by a code of fraud, and the language they speak is lies. (Jn 8: 44) They completely depend upon their ability to mislead, and their strength is measured by how well they can influence, how convincingly they can manipulate our opinions. Truth annihilates them, making their kingdom the most fragile corporation in existence.

As Jesus said, truth, that is the truth of the gospel, of creation, of God's love affair with humankind, sets us free from their world. (Jn 8:32) Although false gods are vicious, their capacity to harm is contained solely in their persuasive skills; they possess no power to destroy anyone who has given his or her life to Christ. Jesus took this authority from them (Rev 1:18) and now they are themselves prisoners sitting on death row, with no opportunity for appeal or parole. Like condemned criminals, all they can do is "write" us letters and "send" us messages.

In particular, these false gods have chosen our minds as their battlefield, and our dominant status as God's children to be the focus of their arguments. If they are able to prevent us from knowing our position, they can stop our personal visions, our pursuit of God, and our connection with and dependence on our brothers and sisters in Christ. Through Anger, Lust and Fear, all the hordes of hell have acted against one prize; that all believing men and women are guaranteed adoption into the family of God.

The evil gods are not really gods at all, but rather slaves to an angry master. We, the focus of their jealous rage, are the offspring of the One who terrifies them. Like earthly children, who inherit the traits and personalities of their parents, we have been endowed with all the authority, all the power and all the wisdom of our Heavenly Father! Like Him, we are impossible to destroy, completely outside the reach of their deadly grasp. To them, and to God, we are GIANTS! Only the unveiling of this truth stands between us and absolute victory. One moment of understanding, one split second of divine revelation will transform everything we have ever known.

When people reach adulthood, and the experiences of growing up have led to addiction, crime, homelessness or mental illness, most believe they are failures. Because success is measured by social acceptance, monetary stability and personal independence, anyone who doesn't display these characteristics is considered an outcast. Even though there are those who believe in restoring the "broken" of our society, the methods used are often patronizing. The person receiving help continues to see themselves as weak, incapable and needy. **Nothing could be further from the truth**.

It is important to remember that there is a constant struggle (Rev 19:20) taking place between God and Satan. Although Satan's eventual demise is clearly outlined in God's Word (Rev 20:10) Satan's hatred and jealousy have blinded him to the facts. He disregards God's sentence of banishment and eternal suffering, doggedly chasing his hunger for domination and control (Is 14: 13, 14) Satan, the "father of lies," (Jn 8:44) has become a victim of his own deception.

Satan considers himself capable of ruling both heaven and earth, and this desire is his obsession. He reminds us of an insecure dictator, who not only wants power, but whose fear of losing it brings him constant worry. This worry, leads to one bad decision after another.   His attacks are unending, but when truth comes and we learn our identity, the tables turn, and Satan soon regrets every lie and assault he committed against us. We realize we are equipped with weapons that, "...are not earthly, but are mighty to the pulling down of enemy strongholds!" (II Cor 10: 4) We have a score to settle!

Because Satan is the leader of his army, he searches diligently for anything that appears dangerous to his ultimate triumph. As an intelligent being, and having been around for at least the past six thousand years, he's become an astute observer of human nature. Satan and his host of demons have made it their job to predict which people might or might not become a threat to their kingdom. In short, anyone who appears to them to be a potential problem becomes a target for attack. This attack begins as soon as the threat is detected. For the GIANTS, the ones Satan considers to be the most fearsome of all, the assaults typically start when they are not yet giants at all, but small children.

"Giants" are the people who Satan sees as dangerous. He gets his clues from their family members (including ancestral lines), their geographical location, their spiritual gifts and their personalities. When he believes a child has powerful, Christian bloodlines, is extremely gifted in the supernatural traits of God, or who has clearly been "planted" in an environment that he considers strategic, he immediately forms a "strike team," a group of demonic forces assigned to stop the child from recognizing his or her greatness and true calling. Anger, Lust and Fear, the chieftains directing warfare against potentially powerful people, are called in to establish the "lie," or "lies" that the child will be told. **Depending on the area of the child's strength, a battle plan is formulated to hide it.** In most cases, the strength the child carries is labeled as a disease, a mental illness, or a flaw in the child's character. Let's look at an example:

One of the gifts of the spirit listed in I Corinthians 12 is the gift of the discerning of spirits. This gift is naturally of huge concern to the gods, as their ultimate defeat comes when they are recognized or exposed. When a child shows signs that this gift is in operation, the strategy chosen against them is usually to label them as mentally ill. Some of these children can hear conversations that to us are inaudible. Some little ones can see the principalities that we can't. Others can feel beings leave or enter a room. All of these sights, sounds and sensations are indicative of the gift of discernment of spirits. People unaware of the spiritual gifting of discernment, including most psychologists and psychiatrists, have mistakenly believed these experiences to be negative and debilitating. Well-meaning "professionals" have conducted vast amounts of research and spent enormous amounts of money in an effort to end these experiences. If these experts were more exposed to the Bible, they would see that the most revered and honored of all of God's people were those who could hear the supernatural realm, see "visions" of what was happening, or about to happen, and feel sensations of God's presence, angelic presence, or demonic activity. In an effort to "cure" people with this gift, the medical world has developed drugs to attempt to redirect thought patterns, minimize emotional responses to these sensations, and increase left-brain "logical" thought. The unfortunate result is that the child is never aware that he or she has a valuable gift. Further, the child is given a label, "schizophrenic," carrying with it a lifetime of inaccurate and damaging self-perception. In Microsoft Encarta Online Encyclopedia 2009, Associate Professor of Psychiatry Kim T. Mueser, B.A., M.A., Ph.D. of Dartmouth Medical School, relates some of the devastation: "About 10 percent of people with schizophrenia commit suicide...people with schizophrenia occupy about one-third of all beds in psychiatric hospitals in the United States. In addition, people with schizophrenia account for at least ten percent of the homeless population in the United States. The National Institute of Mental Health has estimated that schizophrenia costs the United States billions of dollars each year in direct treatment, social services, and lost productivity."

Certainly, when a child is not taught about God, and never given the truth of the gospel, the things they are witnessing not only seem abnormal, but frightening. Their natural reactions to things we cannot see give the appearance of illogical behavior. But the fact that they see things we cannot see, or hear voices that are imperceptible to us, isn't evidence of a problem, but of a gift! Seriously, if we believe there is a supernatural realm, as Christians do, we know there really ARE voices to be heard, entities to be seen, and activities to be felt! But many have been duped by the gods. Christians, non-Christians and professionals alike have fallen victim, and the lie has been proclaimed for so long that we have accepted it as truth. But it is not! If and when the gifted child or adult is finally given the true explanation, the results are amazing. When truth is divulged, this person who has endured a lifetime of pain sees for the first time in their life that they are gifted, unique and valuable. At long last they can believe that God loves them! The relief is enormous, and the bondage of self hatred is broken when they learn that:

(1) Yes, there **are** voices out there, including that of God and of His multitudes of angels, that

(2) What they are experiencing is not a hallucination, and that

(3) There is a divine purpose and usefulness for their abilities!

Chapter Fourteen

WHO YOU ARE
- TRANSFORMING AGGRESSION -
From Anger to Action

*"Do not be afraid of them... for I have given you
victory... not a single one will be able to stand up
to you!"*
Joshua 10:8 (Mine)

The Bible is filled with stories of people who
got angry, and then acted on their anger. The larg-
est percentage of these stories portrays the motivation as positive, and the outcome as victorious!
Ironically, even though we commonly disapprove
of anger, considering it an inappropriate response,
the scripture reveals that the One who got angry
the most was God Himself! Apparently, anger and
sin are not synonymous; anger can be a good thing!

A scripture referred to in Chapter Four, "...
be angry, and sin not," has been greatly overlooked. The fundamental Christian church, while

very committed to the accuracy and authenticity of scripture, has sometimes discounted certain verses, treating them as a personal opinion of the writer, rather than a command of the Lord. But Apostle Paul's words were urgent, because not only did they call for sinlessness, they confirmed that anger was and is a valid emotion! His qualification is only that we handle it correctly.

A teenage shepherd boy, David, in the Old Testament, was furious when a foreign army "defied the living God." (- I Sam 17: 26 - I Sam 16: 14 - 23) This was legitimate anger, yet only a few verses before, the Bible tells us that this same child played music to soothe Saul, a king who was being tormented by an evil spirit; Anger! David's story contains numerous illustrations of both legitimate and evil anger.

Examples are throughout the Word, but perhaps one of the most impressive is the one in the book of John, in which Jesus throws over tables, and literally uses a weapon to terrorize the people He is angry with! He pulls no punches, but screams at them as He chases them out of the temple, the place He cherished as His Father's house, a "house of prayer, not a den of thieves!" (Jn 2: 14 - 16)

One thing becomes very apparent, when reading scripture, that God is a God who is full of emotion. His feelings go the full spectrum, ranging from grief and sadness to joy and pride. Included in this list is anger; Full, horrible rage that causes God to literally regret creating us, and to promise revenge and punishment. If God is truly a loving, doting Father, is this anger a contradiction?

Let's examine what anger **really** is. When something is immoral, cruel, or unfair, we get angry. When something is inconsiderate, rude or distasteful, we become annoyed. We grow irritable when more is demanded of us than we feel capable of. We feel impatient when circumstances delay us, or impede our progress. Are these things wrong, or can anger, annoyance, irritation and impatience actually be appropriate responses?

<u>Anger is appropriate, when it is aimed at unrighteousness</u>. This anger that sees or senses that a boundary has been crossed, is a characteristic given to us by our precious heavenly Father. He gives good gifts, good understanding, and good insight to His children. We're just "chips off the old Block!" Anger only becomes evil when it is borne out of flesh or self-serving desires. Even when it arises to defend another person, it can be motivated by our wish to be admired by the victim, or by witnesses to the event. But anger is not essentially wrong. It is actually a positive, strengthening and admirable characteristic. **It is a motivation to correct injustice!**

A person with anger issues has inherited a trait from the Creator. It is likely that, without a relationship with God, he or she has learned bad habits. Similar to a weapon, anger in the wrong hands, or in the hands of one who has never been schooled in its proper use, is dangerous. (Imagine a gun in the hands of a four-year old!) But anger that is focused, righteous and in submission to God's will is amazingly effective! It, like joy, can create drive in us to overcome, to press through, and to refuse to be denied. Anger can even inspire us to more and longer prayer, and certainly prayer that is more sincere.

When my husband and I were planning our wedding, we spent long hours together at my home working on all the details. One day after he got off work, he arrived while I was in my bedroom. I never heard the doorbell, but one of my children let him in. He often tells this story:

"I came in, and while I was waiting for you to come out of your room, I heard loud talking, like yelling coming from your room. It sounded like you were arguing with someone. I assumed you were on the phone, so I figured I'd better just wait and not interrupt. When you came out, you looked so happy and calm that it kind of confused me, because you had sounded really mad when you were in the other room. But when I asked you about it, you just said, 'Oh, no, I wasn't on the phone. **I was just praying!**'"

Poor guy! He probably wondered what he was getting himself into. He never admitted that, but I still laugh when I think about it. You see, I was telling God exactly how I felt about a certain situation. I don't remember now what I was praying about, but what I do recall is that I had my Bible raised up toward heaven. I was pointing at a certain scripture, telling God that **He** was the One who had promised certain answers, certain blessings and protection for those who were faithful. I remember I was demanding that He keep His Word, and I do recall one specific statement: "God, Your Word says You are not like a man who tells lies, that You don't lie! But if You don't keep Your Word, You are a liar!"

Okay, so I don't recommend talking to God like this unless you're pretty sure there are no dark clouds in the area, or lightning storms predicted. I especially would advise that a person praying this way is pretty clear in the areas of confession and obedience, **<u>before</u>** they start making such bold demands. But when you know that you are meeting God's conditions, and you see things in your life that His Word promises, things you are not experiencing, it really is okay to get angry. Not that He makes mistakes, or that you have to remind your forgetful Father, but it's a good thing to be bold. (Heb 4: 16) God prefers it!

Jesus encourages us to be pushy, too. In a teaching about prayer, He told us to "Ask and keep on asking, seek and keep on seeking, knock and keep on knocking." (- Matt 7: 7) Then He told a story of a persistent woman who was making demands of the town judge. She woke the judge up out of a sound sleep, and wouldn't leave until he finally gave her "justice." Jesus said the judge finally gave in because this woman had worn the guy out with her harassment! (Luke 18: 1 - 8)

When you are dealing with anger, and it has left you in a state of brokenness, loneliness or dysfunction, you might want to reevaluate the problem. As said in the first section about anger, the root problem of unhealthy anger is unforgiveness. Anger that is healthy is not bitter. It merely acts against evil, and once the problem is corrected, the anger ends. Bitterness, on the other hand, is anger that refuses to go away, refusing most of all, to forgive. So what can be done to correct that?

Forgiveness has been oversimplified, especially by Christians. In an effort to find a "quick fix," God's people often rely on a mental decision to forgive as the answer to their bitterness. They choose forgiveness. This is actually a great first step, but it's not the entire solution. A decision to forgive does not create the <u>act</u> of forgiveness. Whatever pain or hurt has occurred, it has often left deep ruts in ones memory and emotions. It has flavored a large percentage of a persons' choices, and influenced many of his or her opinions. Unforgiveness itself literally evolves into an emotional reaction, rather than a clear decision. The path out of bitterness must follow the trail that led us there in the first place. This path is called "Memory Lane," and involves recapturing the pain and the emotions of the original traumas.

When Jesus was on the earth, He had many challenging moments. Religious leaders were a particular annoyance, because they were so convinced they were righteous, and completely closed to new ways of thinking. It wasn't just the pompous Pharisees, though. Even Jesus' disciples questioned His authority and position. To forgive them all, Jesus certainly had to first make a choice. But the Bible records that He went much further than merely making a mental decision, or even expressing forgiveness.

Jesus' most likely moment to forgive, if it was just a matter of choice, would have been just prior to the cross, and before the agonizing prayer that preceded it. It had taken awhile but Jesus reputation was finally established among the people, especially the Jews. After 3-1/2 years of ministry, it seemed that the teaching, the miracles, and probably the consistency of His life had at long last paid off.

He had chosen to return to Jerusalem, where He was quite aware He would be followed, and probably captured by the Sanhedrin. They'd been after Him for some time, and had basically put out a warrant for His arrest. Returning to Jerusalem was risky, but Jesus went ahead, knowing it was God who was asking Him to do so. He asked his disciples to get a young donkey colt for Him to ride on. As He rode through the city center, multitudes of people lined up on the streets, hailing Him as the Messiah! They shouted, "Hosanna, Hosanna," a direct reference of praise reserved only for someone believed to be holy and divine. Knowing He was to die for the sins of all, including these who were worshipping Him, this was the most obvious time for Him to express love and forgiveness. The time appeared correct, <u>because Jesus was in a position to respond!</u> The people were basically admitting that they had failed to recognize His deity, and were repenting. Isn't this the best time to forgive? Not really.

It was later, much later in fact, that Jesus expressed forgiveness. Days had followed, including an arrest, a "mock" trial that really only insulted Jesus further, harsh brutal beatings, and public exhibition and embarrassment. Jesus was battered, exhausted, and in a state of terror. Not many people have ever faced the kind of rage He encountered that day. All the demons of hell had incensed the crowd who had only days before honored Jesus as their Messiah. Shocked and horrified, He could only silently cooperate. The scene was driven by madness, and there was no stopping the wave of hatred hurled at Him.

As the last day of His life came to a close, there was nothing left. Ever felt that way? Knowing this day was coming was of little comfort, for no one could have predicted the horrors of His final hours. He was helpless, drained and enduring pain unlike any we have ever known. Looking down from the cross, He witnessed hatred; the praise of a few days hence had vanished. Now was the time He must choose to forgive. When Jesus hung there, in the most agony a human spirit has ever endured, He could **really** forgive, because if He could do it now, nothing anyone ever did again could resurrect anger, hurt or resentment. If He could feel true love and forgiveness **at the most painful moment of His life**, it could never be questioned. He had to be in contact with His pain, to truly forgive those who were causing it, and He had to have a true grasp on His suffering in order to "let it go." Forgiveness had to be done **in the presence of truth**.

One of the problems with anger is that it sometimes replaces truth. It covers over the memories, almost like a drug designed to disguise our pain. Most people who have been slaves to anger describe it as "acceptable" pain, when they're angry, because it involves choice. The traumas that led to our anger involved events that victimized us, things we had no control over. Anger appears to give us control, and people choose it in the attempt to protect themselves from such events, and from feeling the pain again. When we make the decision to walk away from this god, to stop heeding its signals, to refuse to obey or act on it, we must find the way to healing. Forgiveness brings that healing, and when the wound is gone, there is nothing for the anger to cling to.

Ask God to teach you true forgiveness. He might send you a counselor, or pastor, to walk you through this process. You will have to go down roads you've been avoiding, and trying to cover up with your anger. You will have to bring up memories that you've tried to forget. You'll even have to relinquish depression, self-medicating, and all the "acceptable" ways you've used to stop feeling the pain. You have to come into contact with the pain, the events and the memories to be able to feel and give true forgiveness. It's a heart wrenching process, but there's no other way to heal. It can't be done alone, except after it's been dealt with in the presence and assistance of a skilled, Christian mentor. Later, down the road awhile, you'll learn to forgive quickly, and in the privacy of your prayer closet. For now, though, you are going to need some help.

Finally, when you've chosen forgiveness, learned to wade through the agony of past hurts and trauma, and started feeling the freedom that comes with leaving bitterness behind, you can start to discover why God made you a person who experiences such deep anger. He made you that way. He is that way. He wants you to see that you have reason to be angry, because the demonic realm, including Satan himself, have wreaked havoc long enough. The victims are all around you, and God wants you to be part of the solution! Start asking Him to show you what you can do! Believe me, you're not the kind of person who can stand idly by, watching Satan destroy and devastate the beautiful people God made.

In addition to forgiveness, there is one other key to defeating the god of Anger; Knowing that he is a supernatural force, not a natural one. Natural conditions are the most common cause of the hurt that leads us to anger. Hurt is really what we feel; the anger just comes in through that door. But there are times, like in the personal example I gave in Chapter Two, when anger comes in at the most unexpected moment, almost for no reason at all! Even though it might be invited by a memory, like it was in my case that day, it doesn't <u>feel</u> in balance with that memory. Let me explain. Sometimes, the amount or degree of emotion that comes through anger is much more powerful than what would be justifiable. For instance, when someone you love forgets to call and you suddenly get thoughts of hatred! That is clearly "overkill," (excuse the pun) and you immediately wonder what the heck is wrong with **you**! Instantly, you are aware that these feelings are evil, and way out of proportion. <u>That is your cue, your red flag alerting you to the presence of a force other than yourself!</u> When you recognize that this doesn't even feel normal, it's not! That is the god of Anger, trying to sneak in. First, he might remind you of some event you forgot even happened, or he could capitalize on some disagreement you just had that triggered old wounds. Second, he exaggerates the motive of the perpetrator, and the affect that the event had on your life! "They are doing it on purpose," he whispers, "and they have no respect for you. They're treating you like trash!" That's why we have such violent reactions to small events! We believe there's <u>much more</u> involved than just the present problem! Well, there is much more, <u>much more evil, that is</u>! What you do at this moment is absolutely crucial, and extremely simple. **Call the enemy out!**

When I turned around, pointed my finger, and told the god of Anger to leave, that I would no longer serve him, I could literally feel that thing cowering before me. The most powerful thing I did at that moment was to mention the name of the Lord. I said, "I no longer serve you, or bow to you, because **<u>I bow to Jesus Christ, and Him alone!</u>**" When I proclaimed truth, and the invincible name of Jesus, the god of Anger was exposed, and was forced to stand before the Lord! Now it was no longer me he was attacking, but Jesus, and wow, was he terrified!

Since that day, I have recognized this spirit so quickly that I rarely even address it. When I do, it's just a "reminder," that no, I'm not interested. For awhile, it tried to return, and the encounters were a bit fierce, but I used <u>righteous anger</u>, the anger God felt that I was being attacked, to turn that thing away! When we finally understand that Satan is terrified of Jesus, and of the power of Christ <u>in us</u>, Satan is no longer our problem; we become his problem!

When we come to grips with the devastation around us, and who is responsible ("our battle is not with flesh and blood, but with principalities, with powers, with spiritual darkness and wickedness in high places"- Eph 6:12) we become weapons in the hands of a mighty God. We are moved to action, with the gifts and personality God has given us. We are stirred by compassion and the heartfelt desire to see people free and fulfilled. We want them to see their value, as we have seen our own.

Ultimately, you will begin to love people so much that no one will have to prompt you to act. Action is who you are. Begin to pour over God's Word and find good, wise counsel; learn how to act like Your Daddy! He is excited about you, your personality and your aggressive nature. He needs you desperately, for He uses human vessels to fill with His Holy Spirit. He uses us to activate His army, to lead them. Remember, you have anger, and it is a motivation to correct injustice. Truth, which is found only in God's Word, will teach you what is and what is not just. God has called a warrior back from darkness, and that warrior is you. You are a general in His army. You are a GIANT!

Chapter Fifteen

WHO YOU ARE

- TRANSFORMING PASSION -
From Lust to Love

"You who hunger... with eager desire are to be envied!
You will be filled & completely satisfied; you may weep
now, but soon you will laugh!"
Luke 6: 21 (Mine)

It's no wonder that Paul said he had learned to be "content," in all circumstances. (- Phil 4: 11) This man had a journey of continuous hardship, and only, it would seem, after he gave his life to Jesus! There's no record of persecution, or imprisonment in Paul's life, before his salvation experience. Since he was such a prestigious guy among Jews and Romans, and so well educated, I'd venture to guess he was fairly well off. But once he surrendered to the Lord, wham, captivity, shipwreck, beatings, poverty and incarceration; you name it, he got hit with it!

There are times when we feel like everything is coming against us. It's often at these times that we cry, "Lord, why me?" Like people in the Bible, we complain because our unsaved friends and neighbors seem to "have it made," while we struggle just to pay the bills and have some appearance of a normal life! But "keeping up with the Joneses' " was never mentioned as part of God's plan for us! Jesus even said that he didn't have a place to lay His head; that was part of the "cross" (Matt 16: 24) He was asking us to pick up and carry! And He started that statement with, "Deny yourself...!"

Don't misunderstand. I am no advocate of poverty, and if it was part of the subject of this book, I could give numerous examples of the deceptions that lead to a life of scrimping and scraping by! But monetary wealth or stability is not an indication of God's blessing, in and of itself. Sometimes, it's an indicator of what we're chasing! The root problem of material wealth and possessions is this: we don't own them, they own us! Whether it's a vehicle that needs upkeep, insurance, and a garage to sleep in, or an antique that produces yelling and family fights when the kids touch it, every time you add to your earthly storehouse, you just gained something that you have to guard against, "moth and rust that corrupt," and/or the worry that "thieves break in and steal" it. (Matt 6: 19)

At various times, while shopping for clothes or conveniences, I've caught myself laughing and leaving the store empty-handed, when I realize how many hours my husband or I would have to work to "earn" the item. This brings a bit of reality into my world, when I weigh one-to-four hours of labor against a one-to-four ounce bottle of perfume! Taking it a step further, if I begin to perceive the perfume as a <u>need</u>, because I leave reality, and start living in the fantasy world where "real women" always smell "heavenly," well, now I've got a stronghold in my life, and it's based on a lie! Sure, it might be a small one, but soon, if it goes unchecked, it can lead to more lies. Eventually, "Stuff" gains more and more control over my life.

Lust, as we discussed earlier, is the unhealthy need for gratification. Media is completely enslaved to this god, and their cheesy, dishonest promotion of products they say we <u>need</u> is in direct submission to their idol. The god of Lust is in control, and uses them to manipulate and captivate us. But the misuse of media is not new. Advertising goes back to the Garden of Eden.

The first incidence we see of the god of Lust in action is at the tree of the knowledge of good and evil. Information was the product being sold. (And you thought **<u>we</u>** initiated the information age!) No, that highway first broke ground when Satan told

Eve she could have knowledge like God. Funny, how we serve this god of Lust, in this particular form called "knowledge." People are revered and made famous by their ability to memorize information. We call it intelligence. Yet, if we measure our capacity to learn and retain information against God's, it's more ridiculous than comparing a molecule to the Galaxy! Even so, when we seek to possess it, it becomes an altar for us, where we can never get enough, and we must constantly work and strive in an unending pursuit of more.

But Lust is not all bad. If unhealthy, she drives and owns us. She possesses us, carrying the pink slip to our souls. But when lust, or desire, is righteous and focused on holiness, it begins to drive us over and over into the presence of God! It's not desire that's bad, but it's <u>what</u> we desire that determines if it's good or evil!

Jesus encouraged us to seek, knock and ask. In the last chapter we discussed an illustration He gave of someone who wouldn't stop, refused to give in, and didn't allow herself to give up or surrender <u>until she got what she came for</u>! Sounds like someone with quite a bit of desire, yes? Its real name is **passion**.

A passionate person is someone who others will say is, "tenacious," "not a quitter," "like a pit bull; she never let's go!" Of course, there are many unhealthy people that we describe this way, but the passion in them is not the problem. It's their focus that needs adjustment. Sadly, parents, peers and authority figures are so overwhelmed by the passionate child, friend, or subject that they do all they can to **stop** the passion! They have no idea that this is a gift, given by God. Even Christian leaders make this mistake. Mental health experts, called into the situation long after unhealthy patterns have developed, label it things like, "bipolar," or "manic-depressive." Certainly, the motives behind these efforts are good, at least on the part of the humans. But what's behind their attempts to solve the problem is Satan, who has every intention of putting out the "fire" that burns so deeply in the passionate believer!

Again, like the aggressive person who becomes a victim to the god of Anger, the passionate person, if not validated and mentored, falls prey to the god of Lust. This strong-feeling, hard-driven person becomes like a bottomless pit, trying to "fill" themselves with material possessions, fame and titles, or food and sex. If they are blessed to find Jesus as their Savior, it is likely that the Christian leaders around them will fail to recognize their gifts. This one who has the potential to radically affect his world minimizes himself, even apologizing for being, "hyper," "A.D.D." (**A.D.D.**: *A common acronym of Attention Deficit* Disorder) or "a pest." Never realizing that he's been given the ability to take Satan out, to become the devil's worst nightmare, he cooperates with those around them who constantly ask him to "settle down." So please hear this. Whatever you do, DON'T SETTLE DOWN! If you want to be who God called you to be, get your eyes on what you SHOULD be chasing, what you NEED to be hungry for, the ONE THING that will end your sense of frustration and emptiness. This "one thing" will destroy every evil and insulting word, name or label spoken to or about you. If you do this, you will end the "endless" journey, you will stop the incessant, constant pushing that you've felt. Yes, you were pushing, because you were being pushed. But not anymore!

You are designed, custom built, preciously hand-carved by the Master. You have spent your life trying to fit in, but you were never meant to. Have you noticed that you can't blend with the crowd, no matter how hard you try? That's because God wants you to stand up and be noticed. But you must first chase, run after, and fall in love with the presence of God. You are a worshipper, a lover of His soul, a head over heels, infatuated follower of the Almighty One. You must not heed warnings about fanaticism, but declare, "Fanaticism, here I come!" You were created to be, a 100%, bonafide, sold-out, won't turn back, crazy in love **Jesus Freak**!

If you read the stories of major Bible characters, you will find yourself there, in the pages. Those God trusted were the ones so in love with Him that they would: (1) Obey Him to the point of death, (2) Follow Him to the ends of the earth, and (3) Celebrate Him unashamedly, in the face of religious persecution or threat of torture and cruelty. Some even did this publicly, in their underwear!

None of these people did these things to impress anyone, or even to do something wild for God. They were just like us, not wanting to stick out or cause a ruckus. But when God said, "Do this, **even though** it's radical," He told the ones He knew were just that in love with Him! But first, they spent time with Him.

When you know you're one of these "nut heads," that will basically jump whenever God says, and ask "how high?" on the way up, you also know that you don't want to be misdirected by your passions. The passions are for one thing, to display God's glory. We are in error if the passions bring gratification or glory to us. Of course it brings us pleasure when God is glorified, but our flesh won't experience that sick, selfish feeling. You know the one I mean.

Step one, but not just a step, a life-style, is to spend time in His presence. At home, my husband and I have a room we call, "the Prayer Room." It's just a little tiny space in which we can spend un-interrupted time with the Savior. Whenever the door is shut to this room, everyone in the house knows it's sacred. They leave us alone, and we joke (sort of) with our children, "If there's no blood or broken bones involved, don't knock on that door!" Believe me, my kids don't want to interrupt, be-cause they've seen Mom a couple of times when she didn't spend time with the Lord; eeeeew, yuck, she's not such a great parent without Jesus!

You may not have a room like that. When I was living in a dorm, with four bunk beds to a room, the only prayer closet I had was to throw a blanket over my head! I learned this from Suzanna Wesley, mother of eight children, several who went into ministry. (Ever heard of John Wesley, or Charles Wesley?) Her story reports that they lived in a small house, with only a couple of rooms, so her prayer time was kneeling by a chair in the kitch-en, with a towel over her head. The kids knew, they'd better not interrupt mama when they saw that towel! "Where there's a will, there's a way," they say, and if you're the "passion" person I am, you'll find a place and time with Him everyday. It should be the first thing you do, the last thing you do, and the thing you do when you don't know what else to do! It needs to have balanced shares of verbal, **out loud** prayer, quiet, silent listening, and focused Bible study with a pen and paper to take notes. (Remember, if Daniel, or Jeremiah, or Ezekiel weren't willing to write things down, we'd be missing huge portions of the Bible! God chose them because they **valued** what He said enough to take the trouble to write it down!)

Choose mentors. Don't take the ones who push themselves into your world. They'll remind you too much of that force that's been pushing you. Look for people like your pastor, a seasoned, Bible reading Christian, or even a trusted community figure with a strong, stable ministry. First, ask God for them. **Then** choose them. This ensures the likelihood that they were sent by the Right Source! The Bible says there's "safety in the counsel of many," and a guy or girl like you needs safety, above all things! Focus on listening to advice, and learning to "look before you leap."

Watch out for romantic relationships. These are what you trip on repeatedly, so instead of seeking a mate, seek intimacy with Jesus. The beautiful thing about this method of passion is that, not seeking a mate gives God free reign to decide the person, and the timing. If you seek a mate, that's exactly what you'll get, and all the baggage that comes with it. If you seek God, and His ways, you'll get <u>everything</u> and <u>everyone</u> God intended for you to have; the perfect situations and people, the ones designed for your preciously "unique" personality.

Imagine this. You surrender your desire for validation and romance. You make Jesus your focus. You write Him love letters, say mushy stuff to Him, and start sensing His physical touch, His embrace, even His kisses. You will start to feel contentment like never before. You read Song of Songs, and realize Jesus is madly, romantically in love with you; if you're a guy, this is a real "leap" of faith, to allow these feelings! But after awhile you notice that, although you still <u>see</u> attractive people of the opposite sex, and appreciate them, you feel something godly. You feel love for <u>them</u>, not for how they look, or how they make you feel about yourself! As a matter of fact, you feel so good about yourself that they aren't even making an impact, one way or the other!

Then, one day, you are innocently walking through the park. You're singing a worship song, almost "drunkenly," because you're so enveloped in God's presence. You don't even notice who else is around, you just pray and walk and the emotions lead you to scriptures you read earlier that morning. One of them is, "Seek first the kingdom of God," and you laugh. "Is there anything else, Jesus? I don't want anything else!" Honestly, my friend, that's probably the day you'll run into the person God has been planning for you.

When I first met my husband, I wasn't looking. Oh, I had been looking, so much that it was a complete distraction for me. But I'd learned this something better, this perfectly fulfilling lifestyle of loving on Jesus, and letting Him love on me. By the time Michael showed up, I couldn't have cared less.

I was working in a Christian bookstore, where Michael occasionally shopped. He'd given his life to the Lord, and was there looking for resources to make him stronger in that relationship. I'd seen him there, and at a large church where I attended, and he often visited. He seemed okay, but for one thing, I thought he was married. He thought I was, too, I later learned. Perfect, huh? No pressure, just a brother and sister in the Lord.

One day, shortly after I learned (can't remember how) that he wasn't married, I was standing at the cash register, ringing up an order for him. All of a sudden I recognized something very familiar to me; the presence of God! I'd spent lots of time with Jesus, and I knew what I was feeling. I said nothing to Michael, just smiled and rang up his merchandise. But when he left, I ran back in the storeroom:

"Jesus," I said, "Remember when I told you I don't ever want to get married, that I just want to be with You? Well, I changed my mind. I mean, if **You** don't want me to be married, great, but if You do, if You **absolutely insist**, I mean, if You're really set on the idea of me being married, well, it has to be **that guy!** It's gotta be Him, or I'm not getting married again, ever!" And that guy it was. Six months later, we were married, and I will never, ever be able to thank God enough. I feel so much gratitude, especially that **I** didn't pick my mate!

You see, I wasn't looking for a mate; I was chasing Jesus! But what I felt that day, while Michael stood there, **was** Jesus! It was the presence of God that I'd come to adore so much, and it was the Jesus in Michael that attracted me. That sweet fragrance, that familiar peace, it was all there, and I knew that this man was as in love with the Savior as I was! That was the key, and still is the key, of our relationship. I was running after Jesus. Michael was running after Jesus. One day, Jesus pulled a joke on us. He saw me coming from one direction, and Michael coming from the other, and simply stepped aside for a split second. Bam!

We crashed right into each other. I always laugh, when I imagine Jesus doing that little side step. He must have thought it was hilariously funny!

This example is humorous, but very real. It applies to every material, personal or relationship addiction and drive you've had. You can't lay them down, except at His feet, but if you are in His presence, the god of Lust cannot follow you. You will experience what you've been searching for. When a person, or an object tries to get your attention, run to the One you really want. "In His presence," the Bible says, "is fullness of joy." (Psalm 16: 11) **Fullness**! You'll never feel empty again.

Chapter Sixteen

WHO YOU ARE

- TRANSFORMING DISCERNMENT -
From Fear to Faith

"Stop allowing yourselves to be disturbed... DO NOT give yourselves PERMISSION to be fearful!"
John 14: 27 (Mine)

Although I've never researched this statement, I heard a minister say that the words, "Fear not," were the most frequently repeated words in the Bible! It made sense to me, at the time, and still does; because fear has been at the root of every door I've opened for the "gods." Anger and Lust have crept in as well, but only after the god of Fear came in, sat down, and made himself quite at home! Those precious words, "Fear not," have since carried me through many battles, and out of "hearing range" of the gods! For me, silencing Fear has been the key to shutting all of them out!

It appears that most people, if they are dealing with one, are dealing with all three of the treacherous "trinity." It's a fairly well-accepted fact that someone who appears overly confident is really afraid. In addition, that person is usually fighting with Anger as well, a natural emotion stemming from things that have hurt and frightened them. When they exhibit that anger, it's often driven by Lust, in this case, a lust for power, who has them convinced that attaining a title, position, or strong "rep" (reputation) will protect them, satisfy them and relieve some pressure. Lust doesn't quit there, but returns soon after the "blow up" to lure her exhausted victim into any number of temptations. She calls these "comforts."

The school yard bully and the gods have a lot in common; seldom do any of them act without plenty of backup! Having confronted a bully or two, it's been refreshing to find out how easily they back down! Apparently, those attempting to give the impression of being "scary," are really just good actors. Like "puppets," they're just reading their "lines," and every word is spoken in compliance to Fear. Poor things are more scared than I am! Just as inspiring is the fact that the gods themselves are easily outmaneuvered. By means of knowing our position of righteousness (through the blood of the Lamb) and declaring truth (the word of our testimony" - Rev 12: 11) we almost effortlessly lay our own fears to rest, and this small bit of resistance puts the enemy on the run! (Jas 4: 7) Children learn to protect themselves, when no one else will. Many of those who become violent, aggressive adults are simply struggling with memories of abuse and neglect. Increasingly we see broken parents raising children who become more shattered and devastated than they were. These moms and dads can barely fend for themselves, much less their children. The result is little ones who must cry themselves to sleep after nightmares, dress themselves and scavenge for breakfast, when mom is sleeping off a rough night. Siblings are frequently left to care for and protect each other; sometimes, instead, they attack each other, in an understandable effort to survive. Their morals come from the television set. Their only stability stems from outside sources such as school teachers or care providers, sending them the message that they will never be able to trust anyone in a "close" relationship! Fear, who doesn't get very far with healthy, confident people, makes "road kill" out of these young warriors! While the child is pretending to be tough and independent, he or she is actually trying to silence the onslaught of terrifying threats and predictions; a mental tape recorder stuck on "repeat" replays horrible frightening images and makes bloodcurdling forecasts, day in and day out.

I, like many reading this, will never forget the things that frightened me as a child. The nightmares, which of course were really just <u>symptoms</u> of real threats and abuses, seemed the scariest of all. I believed that I could face anything physical and real, because I could act in self defense, or find a place to hide. But nightmares seemed to be the one event for which I had no defense. Coming at me when I couldn't see them coming meant they could leave me sobbing, trembling, and in a pool of my own body fluids! To make it worse, my sobbing and screaming made my father furious, when the noise managed to wake him from one of his alcohol-induced "comas." Bless mom, though, because she would try to get to me before he did, and give that comforting hug, and reassuring prayer. For every mom who ever ran to her child in the night, I pray the blessing and rewards of the Lord on you; you probably had no idea how amazing that really was!

The experiences of our childhood have led many of us to a lifetime of servitude. Fear has held us for so long, we don't recognize him anymore. Ever been called a "control freak?" Have you ever felt silly about the conditions you needed to relax, to feel safe, or even to feel "germ-free?" What about being overprotective? Even though my mother was such a blessing, I became something more than that with my children. I didn't want them to endure fear, or see the things I had, so I was always preventing what might happen! I didn't just put boundaries around them, I built an impenetrable fortress! Bad guys couldn't get in, for sure, but the kids couldn't get out, either! This resulted in stifling my children's' curiosity, minimizing their creative thinking, and basically making them miserable! Fear convinced me I had the power to stop bad things from happening to my children! Now **I** was the puppet on the string! The truth is, the kids were never mine, and yours don't belong to you. It's Jesus who can protect them, and any effort we make outside of His direction ends in a relationship filled with worry and resentment. We worry, they resent it!

Not everything about my childhood was scary though, and even the moments that were intimidating have actually revealed some interesting abilities I've developed. Survival instincts, of course, become very pronounced in a child who has to learn to use them early. This can come in handy, in the presence of disaster, or at times when circumstances are more out of control than usual. People like us don't tend to panic in emergencies; we've learned to turn off the exterior reaction, and usually make good, solid decisions in a crisis.

Another thing I discovered, that didn't come out of the trauma, but was already there going in, was the gift of discernment of spirits. My mother had been credited by numerous spiritual leaders, with having the "gift of knowledge." It was uncanny how she knew things that were about to happen, before they did. I loved it, as I was proud of Mom anyway, and this "gift" made her seem all the more special. Her gift was used many times to avert disasters in our lives, and the lives of other friends and family. I inherited it, but with me it took on a slightly different and more pronounced manifestation.

Throughout my life, people knew me to be "in tune" with what was "really going on" around me. Even as a child, other children would turn to me for advice; my older sister, six years my senior, even came to me for my opinion on things from time to time. I wasn't especially knowledgeable about world events, politics or scientific matters, but it seemed that the hidden motives and personal character in people read like the front page to me. This was a great blessing from the Lord, but sometimes hindered my ability to "connect" with people that I "felt" things from. Throughout the years, as I grew closer and closer to God, the gift became more refined. He added a bit of wisdom to it, fortunately, that gave me some reserve in discussing what I felt, or exposing everything I was sensing. (If I said everything I felt, I wouldn't have had many friends left! This gift can make you <u>very</u> unpopular, if you don't use it properly!) Whenever I see this gift in others, I always warn them: "Just because something goes through your head, doesn't mean it has to come out your mouth!" (No one listens to you when you give unsolicited opinions and advice anyway; better to keep things to yourself most of the time.)

With this gift came a certain amount of skepticism, cautiousness and distrust. These were unfortunate "side-affects" that emerged whenever I was straying from the Lord, trying to do things my way, or even (gag!) thinking it was MY gift to use the way I THOUGHT it should be used. (Sorry, God!) Most people I've met who give the impression of fearfulness, worry, rigidity, obsessive-compulsiveness, paranoia, over-protectiveness, or are unusually distrusting, are people with the gift of knowledge, wisdom and discerning of spirits. They are "picking up" on "activity" from the supernatural realm, but become fearful when they haven't submitted their gifts to Jesus.

While we are being formed in our mothers' wombs, He blesses us with abilities, and the Bible says He never "takes them away." (Rom 11: 29) The gifts are there, regardless of our relationship or lack of relationship with God. When people report hearing voices, seeing things, feeling the presence of beings that most people don't detect, they are describing a gift of discernment. I always tell those who are just learning about their gift, "You have the right gift, but without the Lord, you're tuned in to the wrong radio station!" This is an expression to show that the gift is still valuable, not to be considered bad or unreliable. We're the only unreliable ingredient, and that's just until we give our lives, and our gifts, to the Lord for His direction and use. That's when all the scary and mysterious aspects of our gift melt away. In the presence of the Holy Spirit, truth reveals that nothing can harm us; we're just outside observers in a spiritual world!

When I was a little girl, my friends watched a cartoon called, "Casper, the Friendly Ghost." He was a cute, chubby, angelic-faced "ghost," very innocent and sweet. He always did good deeds, but was often feared and misunderstood by other characters in the show. I received quite the ribbing when I divulged that this cartoon caused nightmares for me! I was dubbed a "fraidy-cat!" When more television programs emerged about nice witches that did good magic, and wizards that were funny, or silly, they made me very uncomfortable. I was so in tune with the supernatural realm that I completely missed the obvious "point" of these shows, to take the scariness out of such "imaginary" subjects. I was aware of an agenda that the human "creators" of the shows were not; Satan was trying to disguise himself as something cute, innocent and funny. I wasn't even ten-years old yet, when I realized that this was a set up, to get young people used to the supernatural realm, so they could be later drawn into deeper and darker activities, and <u>away</u> from Jesus! I told my mother this, who wisely agreed. This wisdom helped me to grow in a gift, that otherwise made me feel weird and out of place.

Discernment is possibly the most useful of all the gifts. It is truly one of the most reliable sources in the body of Christ, for detecting and preventing fraud and false teaching. If a person with this gift also honors and esteems the validity of God's Word, and submits every "perception" to it, he or she will become absolutely terrifying to the god of Fear. Someone with this gift can completely love an individual, even while knowing that the person's motives or understanding are wrong or incomplete. This frustrates the god of Fear, who wants relationships to be avoided. Instead, the discerner/ lover of people draws others closer, mentoring and ministering to the things they perceive. The god of Fear will suggest that it's "your job" to correct all the things you see are out of sync with love, purity and truth. But our job is not to act, <u>but in knowing, to pray</u>. Because the discerning person is also extremely sensitive, taking action, especially corrective or "political" action or positions, ends up exhausting and breaking them. They aren't built for confrontation. A person of discernment will find themselves being called upon and consulted more and more, as other believers begin to recognize their gift, but the discerning person who is also wise and loving will be very hesitant to "tell all." The damage that can result from "spilling the beans" is often the disastrous "teacher" that shows us how to be more restrained in the future.

People with discernment, but without wisdom, have repeated experiences of utterly destroying Christian relationships, both theirs, and often, those of their peers. This is why it is of extreme importance for the person with this gift to seek wisdom. James tells us that God will give it, "liberally." (Jas 1: 5) Of course, God is anxious to have the reins of our heart, and the steering wheel of our actions and tongues. If we want to take after Him, we should notice that He knows EVERYTHING, but reveals very little! Like Him, also, we need to learn to truly love people, and love His Word. The combination of discernment, properly handling and revering His Word, and loving others is absolutely, hands down the most sure way to bring healing and restoration to this world. We are under orders, after all, and the weapons we have were given to us by the Commander in Chief. No longer do we fear causing harm, once we've been taken through "Jesus Boot Camp." If we take our role seriously, studying His Word, waiting in His presence, and bowing to no other gods, He will release us when we're ready, and the time, His timing, is right.

Remember the famous photograph of the Marines planting the American flag? The movie made from that event, "Flags of our Fathers," depicted the great sacrifices required to be able to raise that flag. You are living that battle, in a spiritual sense, fighting to establish territory for the Lord. In this battle, we too are fighting for freedom, not just ours, but that of so many around us. We have the honor of fighting for the noblest of causes, and will never have to question or regret the wounds we endured, or the scars we still wear. Even our traumas and nightmares have been used for good (Rom 8: 28) to expose gifts God has bestowed on us!

The gods of incarceration, who thought they could hold you, will be disappointed to discover that you have been anointed with the oil of the Spirit. With it, you are slipping out of your handcuffs, and between the bars of Anger, Lust and Fear! They didn't realize that you were getting love letters all along, and that those love letters contained information to help you escape. When you open God's Word, you will find that it is filled with detailed instruction, and lists of promises. Even the gifts you were given are there on its pages. You might not have realized it before, but if you have the gift of discernment, you now know how important it is, and how important you are! The gift you have not only detects the presence of evil, but makes you one of the first to know when the Holy Spirit is around, the first to experience that refreshing breeze, that fragrance. You are one of God's undercover agents. You have weapons that you can carry into the enemy's camp, and use to "pull his covers." You can go in undetected, and release prisoners, set captives free, and open the eyes of those who didn't know, and who couldn't see! (Is 61: 1)

SECTION
SIX

Who God Is

Chapter Seventeen

WHO GOD IS
- THE GIANT LOVER -
Knowing the General

*"Can a new mother forget her baby? Even if that
was possible, I would never forget you! See, your
face is tattooed in the palms of My hands!"*
Isaiah 49: 15, 16 (Mine)

If ever we can really comprehend how Daddy
feels about us, we will no longer struggle with any
of our fleshly notions. So completely fulfilling is
His love that, once we find it, we realize our search
is over. This "Dad of dads," has penned out every
aspect of His heart and personality, in the form of
His Word, the Bible. He "wears" that heart on His
sleeve, and literally bares Himself to us. His desire, His concern, and all His hopes and dreams are
centered on His children; He's like the parent who
has literally lost Himself in His kids! When He
surrendered His own heavenly Son, He was giving
up the Light in Heaven, the Treasure of His Soul.

This exchange is what we point to, when we need reassurance, because we can come close to understanding it as a symbol of His love. But we have yet to fully recognize the enormity of it. The gift He gave is so amazing!

When our Heavenly Father sent Jesus, this is what we got:

Rose of Sharon	Lily of the Valley
Balm of Gilead	Bright and Morning Star
Wonderful	Counselor
Prince of Peace	Light of the World
King of kings	Good Shepherd
Healer	Master
Teacher	Comforter
Messiah	Rock
Ever Living One	Bread of Life
Fountain of Life	Breath of I AM
God's Child	God's Friend
God's Confidant	God's Partner
God's Little Boy	God's Dreams
Life Giver	Righteous Ruler
Lord of lords	Lion of Judah
Holy One	Anointed One
He of Royal Blood	He of Sinless Heart
Captain of the Host	He of Purest Motivation
Alpha and Omega	Promised Redeemer

When our Creator sent Jesus, there were no guarantees, only loose ends and bad odds. God knew we would not respect His Son. He knew Jesus would be shunned, rejected and mocked. He had every reason to believe we would destroy Him, yet He sent Him.

"But God knew the outcome," you might say. "He knew Jesus would be resurrected and return to heaven in victory, didn't He?" Yes, God knew Jesus would triumph, but He also knew the pain Jesus would feel. Here's how much knowing in advance helped God. He knew that the kind of pain that shatters a human mind, devastates a human will, and terrifies human emotion, <u>would be inflicted on His Son</u>. He also knew that no one could take His Son's place. He knew He only had two choices: spare Jesus, and lose us, or send Jesus, and watch in horror. Our God knew that after this magnificent display of mercy, most of us would then ignore the entire Trinity and live our own selfish lives. He was totally aware that, even once we acknowledged Him, it would be a rare day that we would surrender to His plan, or value a relationship with Him. God knew, yes He did, and I challenge anyone to do anything even <u>close</u> to what He did, with as much preparation and foreknowledge as He had. Think about it.

Our Father is a Giant Lover. Although He sends us to the world as tiny, fragile babies, knowing in advance that many of us will spend years in ignorance of His love, He still sees us as "we shall be." He is the ultimate "pit bull," and the undying optimist. He's the Dad in the bleachers, hooting and howling, as one of His children takes even the smallest lead! He is the mentor, patiently teaching us, waiting faithfully when we stray, never ever giving up on us. He watches us when we fall, and is the first One beside us, even when we are cursing Him and blaming Him for our mistakes! More like a doting mother, He brushes us off, cleans our "owies," and applies the bandages of reassurance. He always has faith in us and never stops believing. Rarely has someone referred to as, "Father," ever been so tender and compassionate, yet the General of the most powerful army of all time, is also a sensitive leader, and an affectionate parent.

When Jesus told the story of the prodigal son, the kid that basically blew His father off, abandoned his family, and marched off the property to go "find himself," He was sharing His Father's heart. He knew the love that we were yet to know, thus the purpose for sharing the story in the first place. Although the son in the story failed to value his home, his family, and especially the enormous love of his father, the story doesn't focus on the boy's sin. We see, instead, a dad pacing back and forth, running to the end of the road each day, hoping anxiously for word of his son's well being. When at last the boy finally returns, the story again looks at Dad's heart. The celebration he gives when he gets his boy back is so extravagant that the kid's older brother is even shocked. The elder son hadn't even realized how much his father ached for his lost son. No one knew how much this dad hurt. But Jesus knew, and used this story to show us, <u>it's never too late to come home</u>. He was also making the point that we have nothing to fear.

God is the most explosive power in existence. There is nothing more frightening than God. There's nothing that compares to His strength, or even His temper! Oceans move, skies flip over and the earth rocks off of its axis when this Being is unhappy. Yet all that power is focused on protecting His little ones, His kids. That unprecedented dominance and authority will only assert itself violently against one other kingdom; that of Satan, and the minions that mindlessly trail after him. The reason Satan is the scapegoat is clear, for he is only one irrational enough to come between the Mighty One, and those He loves!

When Satan succeeds in convincing us that we are not so special, that we're "sorry excuses" for human beings, we need to quickly turn to truth.

When Paul recommended we think on things that were, "pure, lovely, praiseworthy, noble, trustworthy," (Phil 4: 8) it wasn't just a Positive Thinking Model! Paul was a strong advocate for reality; to him, truth was everything. This apostle was an expert at regrets, and these words were his own tool for moving forward. He also said that he (and we) should "forget what lies behind, and strain ahead for the prize of the high calling of God." (Phil 3: 13, 14) Instead of replaying memories of past failures and destruction, Paul focused on who he was called to be; the most prominent leader of the New Testament church. Because he was able to grab hold of truth, and the love of His Father, he is still influencing us today. Paul was one of the Giants!

We have a Father who has a message of both tender love and powerful destiny. He is our Commander in Chief, and we owe it to him to pledge allegiance to His kingdom. He desperately loves the people who are walking the earth with us. They are the object of His desire, as we have been. Yet, so many of them have no idea how much they are loved, and how valuable they are to Him. We ourselves are just beginning to understand it, but it can't stop there. We have to turn from our idols and the lies we've believed, if we are to help our Father's cause. Those of us who have suffered, who have been trampled, labeled or rejected, must see that it wasn't our Father who did this, but the enemy. Satan's attack on us has not been any more aggressive than his hostile confrontation against God's Son. We must realize that <u>Satan takes aim at those he fears</u>. But like Jesus, Who was confident in His Father's love and resurrection power, we too can "rise above" the lies of the gods. Every creature, every angelic power, and every saint who has gone before us is waiting breathlessly to see us rise into our rightful places. The Giants have been asleep, lost in foolish nightmares. But they are stirring, waking up. <u>The Giants are about to rise</u>!

Chapter Eighteen

WHO GOD IS

- KNOWING THE RELATIONSHIP -
From Duty to Desire

*"I am a conqueror, a victor (a Giant!) and you will
never convince me, that there's <u>anything anywhere</u>
at <u>anytime</u> that can come between me & God,
or separate me from His Love!"*
Romans 8: 37, 38 (Mine)

Relationship. It's a word that is used, abused
and tossed around like an old, worn out rag. Not
since the word, "Love," has a word been so deval-
ued. I distinctly remember as a child being warned
repeatedly about the things that were "not love,"
because the word was so overused. People were
"in love with" pizza, congregating at "Love Fests,"
and it was "all" we needed, according to the Bea-
tles, anyway. Funny, wasn't John Lennon the one
who "imagined" there was no heaven?

Tragically, the word "relationship" has taken a similar path, and lost much of its intended meaning. We have relationship addiction, relationship classes, healthy relationship, dysfunctional relationship, distant relationships, and intimate relationships. Wow! Sounds like the mainstay of our society! If only that were true. But relationship in its current status has come to mean something like, "duty," or "responsibility." It's like we've become "human doings" instead of human beings! The whole purpose of our creation was to give us the opportunity for an experience, not a job. Work, jobs, obligation; all that came as a result of sin, and anything that looks even close to that needs to be weighed carefully. Although we work, and we do so in obedience to God's Word, it has nothing to do with the original intent He had to commune with us. Like snakes and puppies, work and relationship cannot be compared to one another; they are two different "animals."

First, John Lennon wasn't all wrong. Had he known the Lord, he would have realized where his "revelation" had come from! Although eliminating heaven and hell aren't the answer, Mr. Lennon's observations were valid. He imagined, "...all the people, **living for today**." A bit short-sighted, but one thing Mr. Lennon saw that we often miss is that life can quickly pass by us, if we don't pay attention to the present. He saw that many people were either lost in the past, or lost in concerns about the future, so much so that they weren't enjoying anything they were doing **right now**. This "right now" attitude is an important key in relationship, especially relationship with God.

In John chapter 12, we see a precious example of someone who understood that Jesus was with her for only a "short time." This obviously concerned her. Mary, sister of Lazarus, is said to have had a bad reputation. The Bible doesn't clarify, and women back then could gain a bad rep from any number of issues. Whether it was health issues, problems with submission, or some kind of promiscuous behavior, we don't know. But Mary was one of the Giants, of that we can be sure.

When Jesus joined his friends for supper, and as he and the disciples were awaiting the preparations, Mary came in to the room where he was sitting. This was probably frowned on, as in another gospel, we learn that her sister was really upset that she wasn't in the kitchen, helping cook the meal. Poor Mary! Love had blinded her, and caused her to make a purposeful decision to "buck the system." She did so, because she understood that Jesus' earthly journey could soon end. She felt an urgency to spend time with Him. When she came in the room, she sat at Jesus' feet and wept over Him. She had some valuable oil with her, something apparently rare and expensive. It seems she knew exactly what it was for. Later criticized for "wasting" it, Mary emptied the vial over Jesus' feet. Now it was customary to bring water and towels in, to wash the feet of a guest, a refreshing act of respect that eliminated mud and grime. Mary was not a "halfway" kind of girl, though, and her extreme passion, that would probably have gotten her on some kind of medication these days, drove her to use the most precious substance she had, for the sake of her first love. Jesus was all she knew, all she wanted. To Mary, there was no other purpose for the perfumed ointment; it existed for Him, and so did she! She revealed a heart of total devotion when she cleansed His feet with the perfume, and then dried them off with her hair!

Mary was a lady of passion. As we learned in one of the chapters about Lust, this spirit "targets" this kind of person in an attempt to warp his or her passions. Lust lures them, bringing every kind of material possession, position of respect or physical and emotional gratification into view. The spirit itself pretends to have the best of intentions. It gives the appearance of being concerned, desiring only to bring us comfort. The real reason it pursues us? Lust knows her only chance to prevent us from "pouring out," from "emptying" ourselves for the Lord, is to distract us. Once we get sight of

Jesus, and experience His awesome presence, we will never be satisfied by anything else. Like Mary, one taste and we're hooked!

Our relationship with God is the ultimate high. It takes us out of our troubles, out of our selfishness. When we get close to Him, we find ourselves in another dimension. This is why food, drugs, alcohol and sex hold us, because they give a temporary feeling that "takes us out" of our immediate concerns and failures. They, of course, are counterfeit "highs," poor, weak substitutes for the blissful, eternal state of being we find when God's Spirit enters our world. Using the ammunition of past traumas or future fears, Lust doesn't ever give a promise of healing; only forgetting. She gives us a few minutes or hours of deception, to help us escape.

In relationship with Jesus, we discover that we can now, right now, in the middle of any situation, escape. Without shirking our responsibilities, we can bring them, instead, to the Savior. I laughed the first time I read the verse in John 15, where Jesus told the disciples, "Apart from Me, you can do nothing!" "No kidding," I thought. "In my case, Lord, I don't even want to try!" This came from the revelation that anything I could do well, He could do better through me. If I would allow myself to surrender control, placing absolute trust in

Him, I could practically become <u>irresponsible</u>! In a sense, I could shove all my problems on God. Even though I might still go through the motions of taking care of the situation at hand, I was really free of the load! He said His burden is light, and so I habitually dump anything that feels heavy to me <u>on Him!</u> If things turn out well, or don't, it's no longer my problem, because I didn't create the plan for my life, nor do I need to come up with the ideas for what each day should hold!

Further, by looking back at my "track record," I can honestly see that the mistakes I make are usually part of what makes the plan successful. Yes, God knows my unique, if not quirky nature, knows I'll do and say things that get me in all kinds of hot water, and He uses that to get me <u>across to the other side</u>! (Can you picture that? I fall into the "hot water," and God yells, "Swim!") Even my brushes with the law, my opinionated decisions, my disrespect for others, have all forced me into situations in which I found Jesus!

Mary valued Jesus' presence more than anyone else in the room. That's saying a lot, because those in the room were Jesus' disciples, and His best friends. But Mary was the one who treasured Him more than her reputation, more than money, more than comfort. I think it's because of this that Jesus appeared to Mary first, before anyone else, when He resurrected from the dead, Her longing for Him drew Him to her! He looks for those who desire Him, who ache for His touch!

It's vital in our relationship with Him to love and esteem the present moment. That moment, that place of prayer and meditation before we start our day transforms everything else. Nothing else can dominate our thoughts, when we are in His presence. David said in the Psalms, he would "dwell in the house of the Lord forever." (Psalm 23: 6) He knew and treasured "the moment." Like much of what David said, this was a prophetic statement, referring to the position we now have of being "the house of the Lord." Yes, we **are** that house, the "temples" of the Lord's dwelling, and can be in that place with Him all the time. But we have to reach into that place to truly "dwell" there. We might not do things correctly; we might say things we wish we hadn't. The key is to know where to run, and to do it quickly and often. Going to the chamber, where we give ourselves permission to weep, is where we also find a God Who responds. Running to the secret place of our soul is the way a giant becomes aware of who he or she really is. It's in God, as we look into His face, that we see ourselves. Knowing we carry that place within, we can be confident and at peace in the "now" moments, when everything outside of that place is unreliable.

In prayer, I often imagine God's face. Like the face of a person who loves me, I visualize His soft expression, <u>and the reflection of me</u> that I see in His eyes! That's where I "find myself," not in some material object, or some claim to fame. I don't find **me** when my physical body gets filled with food, or mind-altering chemicals! As a matter of fact, the "me" is the part I'm trying to escape, with interruptive thoughts, or with a fantasy "me," something created in my mind. Unfortunately, when I come back to reality, I still see the same person staring back in the mirror. When I'm with Him, though, I never, ever see false hopes and dreams. I don't see illusions, but total validation of who I am.

One of the most precious things God ever spoke to me, when I was listening (because I spend at least half my time with Him listening) was when He said, "Kim, I <u>like</u> your idiosyncrasies. I like the things about you that you think are odd. I made you that way ON PURPOSE! Those are the things I needed in you to make you effective in ways and places where others can't be. And trying to hide them just brings shame; just allow yourself **be** yourself!"

Wow, what a day that was, and what a liberating memory it still is for me. You can see why I like hanging out with Him! When I look in that face, I see that He and I together can be complete. I, without Him, am nothing. I love that. It doesn't make me sad or upset. I cling to it; because it puts <u>every worry, every failure and every lack</u> I have into proper perspective. These things become subservient to me, and to the plan God has for me. No longer do they control me, but I them. When the mistakes occur (yeah, when **I** happen) it's quite possible no one around me will understand. I almost never understand, and become frustrated with myself. But, when I run to that place, that safe, familiar "closet" with Him, I quickly experience healing. Immediately, a plan begins to formulate, and a "reconciliation recipe" or an insight leads me to wiser decisions. Most of all, I can see, because instead of staying "under the circumstances," where the load is more than I can bear, I now find myself sitting on Daddy's shoulders; from here, I can see over the top!

That day of revelation was probably one of the first steps in being able to understand how God feels about the Giants. Through my own missteps God was able to show me all the things that these false gods have tried in my life, to pull me away from Him. My screw-ups were just things He allowed so I would see <u>their</u> wicked devices, and how badly I needed His help. He let them "overplay their hand," so to speak, doing things so awful and devastating, that I would have no doubt who was behind it all. He simultaneously was showing me that the things in me that man has labeled as flaws were the gifts He placed in special "agents" created for special purposes. It was the extremes in me, the ones man thought needed to be controlled or eliminated, that God wanted to use. It was the depths of depression that forced me to cry out, and those dark moments became sessions in which He and I began to plan and strategize. It was in those pits that I saw the devastation of those around me, and it was the anger I felt at what Satan had done that created the energy to rise and fight. In the places of fear, I saw entities that many would have called illusions. Had I confessed, I would surely have been put on medications. And it was the strong pull toward intimacy that God used, and continues to use, to draw me to Himself.

Because this urge is so overpowering, I find myself an "addict" to His presence, and often beg for His touch. A prayer I pray often is:

"Jesus, You asked Your Father to manifest Himself to us. People say we should, 'walk by faith,' and they seem to mean we don't need to <u>feel</u> anything. But I do! 'Manifest,' comes from the same root word as 'manual,' meaning to use your hands. Jesus, I need Your Father's hands to touch me, and since You prayed it, and I am agreeing with it, I'm asking for that touch NOW!"

This prayer has never failed to meet my need. Although my words change a bit, I carefully use God's Word in this and most prayers, to bring evidence to the Lord that I am counting on His promises, and not only that, I am making a demand. My loving God seems to enjoy this boldness, and He comes to me faster than the wind. I am instantly filled with His presence and waves of His embrace sweep over me. The experience sometimes makes it difficult for me to go back to my day to day activities; I often cry and plead with Him saying, "God, I don't want to leave." But I do leave, because there are precious people out there that need to know this love. They need us, and although some will never listen, we must do all we can, and **be** all we are called to be, in the hopes that some will. Even the ones I don't understand are, like me, created uniquely, designed intentionally.

This chapter was perhaps the hardest to write, because my relationship with God is too deep to put into words. Expecting you to read and develop your relationship with Him, based on my words, seems almost too much to ask. Yet I must trust the Holy Spirit to reveal to you that the relationship you have with Him, not anything you do, but what you are and feel with Him, is the only thing I can share that means much at all. I have an overwhelming desire for you to see who you are, and the only way you ever will is by getting really close to Him. Through His eyes, you will not be transformed, but see what is already formed. Ever hear the phrase, "Love is blind." Well, it's not, because love and truth are characters of God; they aren't blind, but rather, they see what's really there! What will transform, in His presence, is how you see yourself.

When you realize all the lies you've been told, as He reveals them to you, you'll rise out of those moments ready for battle! When you see through His eyes, the truths that you can hold on to, Fear will run in terror; Fear will fear you! Lust will vacate the premises, having no more influence in your life, for you will feel complete. Anger will melt in the presence of forgiveness, when you understand that it was the other giants, the ones who didn't understand God's love, who were deceived into hurting you. You might even go back and get them!

Let your heart melt in Him. Let your heart trust in Him. Let your heart be His, and don't look back. It's not a man/woman romance. It's much higher, much deeper. It's not a sick, emotional feeling that comes and goes, but a sense of purpose and honor that gives meaning to everything past, present and future. Let your feelings out, in His presence. Let your plans drop at His feet. Let all other relationships fade in comparison to what you have with Him. Become the giant, the warrior you were called to, and walk away from the lies.

As Christians, we are ensured victory. Everything in the Bible points to our need for intimacy with God, and the purpose of going to battle for Him, and for His intended outcome. Since we are told that we are not in a human-against-human battle, but one in which we encounter spiritual forces, we need to know who those forces are. They've known about us for a long time, and it is reasonable to believe they would try to destroy those who would fight the hardest, be the bravest, and last the longest. That's where you come in, and knowing that strategy, should tell you something about Satan's opinion of you. He's the little general who is looking for people like you, that he considers a worthy opponent. His tool is to separate you from intimacy with God, because if he is successful, you'll never, ever see yourself through the loving eyes of your Father. If you don't see, you won't stand, and if you don't take a stand, your life is meaningless. Without meaning, you will not survive. Without God, you have no direction, no place of restoration and no reason to live.

If, however, you do discover that place in His arms, that "safe zone," where lies cannot reach you, you will never stop being thankful. Your life will become that vial of perfume, poured out because it's the most you can do. Once you find your heart filled with His love and mercy, nothing else will matter to you. You'll change the world, every time you venture out into it. You'll change the atmosphere, because the enemy will scatter when you show up. You will always be a leader, as you are now, but finally, your influence will bring people to their destiny.

The gods are in a meeting, right now, as you read this. The last thing they want is for you to know who they are, because with that knowledge, you will now begin to recognize their tricks. They're in that conference room, trying to figure out a way to get you off of this "truth" stuff! But believe me, they won't succeed. You only need to decide that it is the truth; knowing it is will set you free! (John 8: 32)

As I said before, Satan has been your problem long enough; it's time that you turn that around! Rise up, as I did, and make it "payback" time. When the Bible says vengeance is His, that He will repay, don't be surprised when He starts using you to do it! Don't look for a fight with mankind, for they are the objects of our Father's affection. But don't ever again sit back and watch things happen; make them happen! Go after the enemy, and whenever you recognize him, confront him! He cannot stand in the face of love, of truth, or of worship. You have these weapons, and more. Let them pour out of you, as the old behaviors used to. Be angry, but don't miss the mark of what that anger is for! Let desire overtake you, but let it be for God and Him alone, because **that** relationship is worth more to you than anyone, or anything. Fear only that His presence, His spirit would be taken from you. (Psalm 51: 11) Fear nothing else. Giants, awake!

SECTION
SEVEN

Stomping Their Feet

Chapter Nineteen

STOMPING THEIR FEET
- PURITY AND PRIORITIES -

*"Whoever cleanses himself from contamination is
now a container God can use;
God can use a person like this for anything!
Philippians 4: 8 (Mine)*

We have been agreeing with false gods. We didn't know it, but once it's revealed, it makes us angry. Why didn't we realize it? How did we fall for it? Now is not the time for self-accusation, though, because that's just another one of their methods, remember? We are not condemned, (Rom 8: 12) but free, and we have no time to waste!

By looking at Jesus' words in Matthew 24 (Matt 24: 4 - 14) and comparing them with other prophecies in the Bible, it's obvious that time is of the essence and thankfully, we might have some left! We just don't know how much. Really, from what the Lord has revealed to me, it seems that the wait, the period of time we didn't "get it," was all part of the plan, too. Even though we have experienced heartache, we have also grown, and we have seen our <u>desperate</u> need for God. This awareness is the key to flipping things over, to turning our grief into power! Being part of an army that's been "sound asleep" might seem like a bad thing, but it's really not, because the army was hidden "for such a time as this." (Esther 4: 14) Now is when we are needed the most, and had we known before, when our numbers were smaller, or had our gifts been recognized and utilized more commonly, perhaps we could not have made the overwhelming impact that God has held us back for! Even the frustration of having been deceived is a driving force in us now, drawing us together in unity and opening our eyes to see each other with respect. That respect will be crucial to receiving the blessing of the Lord, because it's when us "brothers" dwell in unity (Ps 133: 1) that His word says He is attracted to us, and it was when the disciples and followers of Jesus waited, yes waited, were held back for a time, in the upper room, learning to dwell together, to get along, to show honor to each other, when that happened, wow, the Power of God showed up. There were more saved that day, through the bold words of one rough, angry fisherman than on any other day recorded in scripture! Know why? 'Cause Peter, that guy, and the others with him in that room found out who they were! (Acts 2: 1 - 4, 14, 41)

Once we give our lives to God, and silence the false gods in our lives, we have a completely new agenda. What pleases God? That becomes the question, not just daily, but throughout the day. What am I thinking about? Is it the truth? We start evaluating our thought patterns, filling in the ruts and ditches where old lies held us, taking higher ground as we enter a completely new battle! We start realizing that there is nothing else to do but rise up! We are defiant, and we are stirred by passion to see others set free. When we look at someone we previously hated, we see them as broken. We feel compassion for those we were once disgusted by. We approach people, with our heads held high, not because we're "all that," but because we know now why we're here!

I, for one, am unwilling to allow apathy to keep me directionless. I have allowed anger to rise, and I stand beside an angry God. I have allowed myself, even in the writing of this book, to share scripture-validated principles that are both exciting and risky. But for me, the only thing truly risky is to keep quiet, especially if this message will wake up an army that has enough guts and history to know that Satan is a powerless peon whose time is up!

I have felt, seen and heard things, things that I've read in the Word, but that seemed disconnected and unrelated, until now. I knew that material things or people could be perceived as idols, even though the book of I John clearly states that it's not just "people and things," but "**any**thing" that takes the place of God in your life that is a false idol. (Heb 10: 25) Now I see what I never did before. I have bowed to the enemy. But now I know that I have to walk in truth, and get my priorities in order, especially after so many wasted years.

God is first. Of that, we have no question. We used to believe the things that were said about us, but now we can see that the one Being Who represents truth, really believes in us! That makes Him first, automatically. Then, my family is second, because the Word says so very much about how horrible it is to neglect your spouse or children, (Mal 3: 10) and Paul even said that having your family well managed and healthy was a prerequisite to ministry. (I Jn 5: 21) That meant, family had to be working together as a team, with everyone's needs met. Third, because I can hide so much of myself when I am ashamed, I need to expose myself instead. I need to connect with the body of Christ completely. In Hebrews we're told that we should gather together more and more, as the "day," the end of days approaches. (I Tim 5: 8) My own church is where I'm supposed to serve and tithe (I Tim 3: 2 - 5) and also be exposed and "called" on my "stuff." I can wander the streets all day, preaching about Jesus, but none of those   people are gonna know if I'm living what I'm preaching! My pastor, however, and the people I get close to can keep me accountable. What's really awesome, too, is that the ones that know God's word are going to encourage me to go higher, and get closer to God! Finally, when I am released, like the way Paul told Timothy to release people into ministry, I can take this stuff anywhere! The secret to keeping all of this straight is this: be humble before Jesus, spend that time with Him, and listen. He tells us when we're blowing it.

The voice of the Holy Spirit, Jesus said, would convict us of sin. (Jn 16: 8) This is really important, because sin isn't breaking a rule or a law. Sin is anything we do that defiles our love for God or for people. But, like the sheep we talked about before, if we can learn to hear His voice, by waiting, listening, and comparing what we think we're hearing to God's written words in the Bible, we will have found step-by-step instructional living! No one person has all the answers, yet God speaks through believers too. The Bible says there's safety in the counsel of many. (Prov 14: 6) When we allow the "many" to speak to us, and take it back to Jesus for his comments, we come out with detailed patterns, guidelines, and corrections! There's no confusion, either. Since we're allowing those corrections, even through people who don't "look like much," (like, sometimes, our kids - Ps 8: 2) and we're taking it all back to God, we can't go wrong! Well, not real wrong, anyway.

You'll still mess up, but God won't push you away, like you thought He would. He'll probably laugh. I think sometimes when I mess up, He looks over at some of the angels in heaven and says, "Can you believe she did that again? She's so funny!" Then He picks me up and says, "Okay, so are you just gonna sit there? Don't let that little thing stop you! Make corrections, my dear, and then GET MOVING!"

Mostly, as we put God first, we won't allow much to get in the way of what He wants. It's kind of simple, really, because it's like we've found what we're looking for, and no one's gonna take it away! You won't see temptation like you did before; it will disgust you. No, YOU won't disgust you, but that person you were, that was so dark and ugly will repulse you. You won't want anything that looks the slightest bit like that person. When you feel that "old man" in you rising up, it will be minutes before you're on your face before the Lord. And again, He just wants you to correct it, not beat yourself up. But the constant return to drugs, alcohol, food binging, perverted sex, violence; all that won't be part of you, even if you have fallen thousands of times before. You just have to decide what's truth.

One more thing about purity and priorities. There are two voices: One is the voice of the Holy Spirit. The other is the voice of the enemy. Both of these voices will tell you when you sin. It's really important that you know the difference between how they sound!

When Jesus, through the Holy Spirit, comes to me to confront me about something, <u>He is always kind</u>. Even when He's firm, and sometimes He's had to be REALLY firm with me, because I'm pretty stubborn, He's still not critical, disrespectful or ugly about it. It's like He sticks out His hand and says, "Come with Me. We need to talk." If I avoid Him when He does this, I start having anxiety. Picture it this way. I start to walk away, God sticks out His foot, and trips me! Wham! Nothing's going right. That's a warning that I'd better go work the stuff out with Him, that He's not kidding. If I continue to ignore Him, Hebrews says there's "no sacrifice left," for that kind of sin. (Heb 10: 26) I'm in real trouble now. If I don't repent, I'm on my way out! Still, the voice I hear from the Spirit of God is telling me that, even though I'm wrong, everything will be okay. He tells me that it's just an error, not to get "stuck" there, but by all means, turn around!

He forgives me so quickly, that it blows my mind! The Bible says He throws our sin into the depths of the sea. (Micah 7: 19) He sees me as innocent all over again! That's how it feels when God tells me I've fallen.

When Satan, through his mini-dragons, decides to remind me of something I've done that's evil, he doesn't exactly add any mercy. He makes me feel like a total loser, and adds criticism and put downs. I start feeling like giving up, like it's not even worth trying, because I'm so messed up. <u>That's because those are the words I'm hearing</u>! Remember the statistics on people diagnosed with schizophrenia, that <u>about 10%</u> commit suicide? <u>That's because those are the words they're hearing</u>! We don't come up with this stuff, Satan does.

When you start feeling like there's no hope, that all the promises in God's Word, and all the sense you had that you were part of His plan, are really for other "better" people, know it, friend, you are hearing the voices of the gods! They have swooped in to condemn you. That's their job, and they do it well. ANYTIME you feel like packing it in, that is absolutely, hands- down, without a doubt those familiar voices that messed you up in the first place. You have to know they are liars. So what to do?

CONFRONT THEM! I do, and felt a little weird the first time. I saw right away, though, that what I'd seen in God's Word about their schemes, their stealth patterns, their lies; it was all true, and they were real! When I'm scared, even just worried about my busy schedule and demands, I tell Fear to leave! I've been doing this for years, and not only do I recognize their voices, they recognize mine too! When I feel Anger taking over, especially when it's directed at another human being, I tell Anger that those are God's creations, people He adores, and I absolutely refuse to think, feel or speak anything bad about them. When I feel the need to receive gratification of any kind, now, I tell Lust, "You know what? You are an old idol in my life, and as far as I'm concerned, DEAD! My treasure is Jesus, and you can't offer me that! He's not even on your menu."

In struggling with these things, I use God's Word to remind myself to be slow to anger and quick to listen so I can sort out the truth, to "fear not," because Jesus has my back and to focus on the prize of bringing people to Him, which is waaaay more satisfying than anything Lust can offer me. Well, that's what I do. I really, honestly speak to those entities OUT LOUD, when they're really bugging me. I have no problem getting in their faces, because they are losers! They are also cowards, and they're scared of us!

God's Word is so full of ammunition, too. Like in the description of God's armor (Eph 6: 15) it speaks of our feet being covered (like with shoes) with the preparation of the Gospel. That's God's Word! Now keep in mind that our feet are the first part of our body to experience a place we're going! That's right, when you <u>step</u> into any situation, your feet touch it first, right? So if they're covered with God's Word, everything we experience has to first pass the Bible test! (Imagine wearing "Bible" shoes!) We filter everything through the truths in God's Word, kind of like when you run something by a reliable friend! Truth sifts out the lies, and steers us toward solid ground. (When we don't use God's Word to "test" things, we might end up stepping in something awful!)

Another aspect of this "word picture" we're given, is the way it shows God's Word as the weapon we use to defeat the gods! First it refers to His Word as our sword, and then to the gospel, or the good news as our boots. Like a sword, scripture is portrayed as an aggressive, offensive weapon that we carry at our side to go after and destroy the enemy. Like steel-toed boots, scripture is then depicted as a covering, protecting us as we march forward! We chase after the ones we can see with our sword, and trample the ones that get in our way. "The God of peace crushes Satan under our feet!" (Rom 16: 20)

As we utilize our weapons, and CONFRONT the lies that roll around in our minds, we will become the most powerful army this earth has ever seen. You see, we were broken, because God allowed it, and because of it we have become seasoned warriors. As the world gets more and more evil, seasoned warriors are exactly what the church will need to defeat the enemy. We who have seen darkness, who have survived evil, and who have fought for all the wrong reasons, are the forces God wants to use to deliver the people He loves! The average church-goer today doesn't know real battle like we do. There are some amazingly wonderful people in the church, but so many of them have sat there just a little too long. Their motives might be good, but they've become sedate and presumptuous. Unfortunately, the church is under spiritual hypnosis right now, very content to live average, low-profile lives, being "good" Christians. When all hell breaks loose, it's going to hit them hard, and they are our brothers and sisters!

You, my friend, have been chained long enough. It was the only way Satan could deal with your power and energy. But God is breaking the chains, the lies you believed. <u>He is breaking the chains of many, all at once</u>, because all of the evil that will be unleashed is in the starting gate. You, and the other giants, are the ones that God needs to lead this battle. The other Christians, the ones that seem to have it together, won't even know what hit 'em. They'll be looking to you. One thing, no matter how they've labeled you, or minimized your calling, when Satan's dark principalities are set loose, and every disgusting, terrifying demon is mobilized to steal, kill and destroy, the church will recognize you; <u>then</u> they will see a warrior!

Christians and society as a whole have seen those of us who have been "broken," as just that. To them, we're what "could have been, if only." Like Green Berets, or undercover agents, <u>we have been intentionally hidden from the eyes of all of mankind</u>. This was purposed by God, so we would not be given away. But now, God needs to reveal who we are, because even though it's a "heads up" to the enemy, God wants the church to know what's going on. The Bible says nothing happens without God telling his prophets first. (Amos 3: 7) Fortunately, Satan's not usually the first to believe it anyway, so most of what God does completely blindsides him! But the church, God's people, needs to know we're here for them. They won't make it without us. Like lambs to the slaughter, they desperately need protection and guidance. We need them, too, because they have much wisdom and compassion to help us through "basic training." We're not completely ready, but we can get ready quickly. The only thing holding us back is our cooperation with old lies, telling us we're not much. WE ARE MUCH!

I pray you pass this on, too, because now you know who the Giants are. I don't have to spell it out anymore than I already have. The Giants, those who were labeled, or locked up, or tossed out in the street, they know each other well. For hundreds, maybe thousands of years, we have been a family. Were we dysfunctional? Yes, but never was any force truly able to divide us, and even society around us sees us as one. When we get up, we will rise together, and the world will be shaken to its foundations. Men, women and children will be astonished, even frightened, until it becomes clear why we rise. Those we misled, harmed or deceived will change from opponents to allies, when they see what God saw all along! We are the passionate, aggressive and the discerning last-day throng of power and righteousness. We need to be the leaders we were called to be. If we answer the call, the world will change overnight, because it will be the first time in history that such a huge army will suddenly and uniformly take their places. For once, and for all, we will lead all who are willing to the place where we ourselves were transformed; we will lead them to truth, at the feet of the General!

As I close this chapter, I recognize what a friend pointed out, that some of you will not see each other with respect. Still, and I know this is true, we have prejudice and false notions about people who are different than us. This is our last chance to put that behind us. May I warn you? As one who has been labeled "different," I have learned to see people's hearts with the microscope of the Spirit. I have learned to dig out the treasure, because I was blessed with a revelation. It was this: that every person who has been identified with any kind of label is one of the Giants. Here's what I found in scripture the other day. It's a story I've always been able to relate to.

David was running from King Saul, because Saul was jealous of David. David was promised to be Israel's next king, for one thing, and then he became very popular with the people. So Saul hated him, and David spent many years running from the guy. Wow, do I know how that feels. I hate jealousy, and when God asks me to "stand out" in any way, I usually expect the worst. I've learned, now, that God created me to stand out, so I've quit trying to hide.

David went to a priest who was one of King Saul's subjects. Apparently, this priest was fond of David, too. David asked him for prayer, and he also asked if the priest had any weapons laying around. David had taken off in a hurry, and had no arms or ammunition with him. The priest presented him with the sword that David had taken in his first famous victory, the battle with Goliath!

David traveled on to find refuge with another king, in Gath, one he thought was a friend. But the king's servants told the king that David was there to overthrow his kingdom. Now David was in danger again. When he heard about the rumor going around, he cleverly pretended to be insane, drooling on himself, and writing weird stuff on the walls of the city. Just as he planned, everyone thought he was out of his mind. They let him go, thinking he wasn't capable of harming anyone.

David escaped to an area in the wilderness, to a cave called Adullam. His brothers and all of his relatives heard where David was hiding out, and went to join him. David's reputation for being blessed by God, and being a great military strategist must have gotten out too, because the Bible says that everyone who was "in distress, or in debt, or discontented," began to make their way to his side. He soon had an army of 400 men, men who knew they'd found a guy they could follow. But why did they follow David?

David was like you. He stood out. Even when his own dad, Jesse, said he was just a "shepherd boy," the youngest kid in a family of tough, experienced soldiers, a priest named Samuel saw David with the microscope of the Spirit. God had called him to be king, and Samuel heard the voice of the Lord say, "This is the one I want." David's life was never the same, from that moment. Even though he was just a young teenager, he was soon perceived as a threat to Saul, who ruled in Israel, and the leaders of all of Israel's neighboring countries. Every person who had or desired power, felt threatened by him. He became one of Israel's "most wanted," and that reputation spread even to foreign countries! He was just trying to stay alive, yet everywhere he went, he found enemies he never knew he had!

David's gifts, and anointing, had frightened Satan. The Bible said that he had a "heart after God." We know, from studying David's life, that he was a musician and a worshipper. Although life had not put him out front, God had. His family even thought of him as just a kid, and had put him out on the "sheep" detail, instead of giving him anything really important to do. But David had done his duty with his whole heart. He'd gotten so good at killing lions and bears, that when he looked at Goliath, a trained soldier twice his size, he wasn't even afraid. David had gotten confidence, while out there in the hills. He'd become an expert with a slingshot, and said he'd even killed some of the animals attacking the sheep with his bare hands! He'd been through battle, alright, and even when no one seemed to see him as powerful, God did, and so did Satan.

One of the things that made him extremely worrisome to the devil was his passion. First, David was passionate about God. He bragged on God, sang to and worshipped God, and prayed long and loud. Those lonely hours in the hills had paid off, because David and God had become tight! Nothing about David's human toughness and confidence scared Satan nearly as much as this. David might have been unnoticed by people, but he stood out in the spiritual world!

David was a survivor. As the youngest kid, his culture labeled him as the least valuable. He was basically the invisible child, who was the last to eat, the last to get a gift, and the lowliest in the order of inheritance. David didn't let this keep him from becoming the greatest at whatever he did. David was passionate, too. If David lived today, he would have been the kid in third grade who was asked to guard the teacher's desk, while she was out of the room. When the teacher returned, she would have found her desk surrounded by a circle of chairs, and David standing between the desk and the other kids, with the yardstick held out like a sword! The other kids in the room would have been held captive in their seats, afraid to move for fear David would beat them to death!

David was a man of passion, insanity, mood swings and violence. But he was also a man of integrity and undying love for God. In writing the Psalms, David shows us he was a man unashamed to cry, and who ran to God for everything. No one ever doubted where David stood, and those who were discontent, who later followed him, found what they were looking for. Criminals and the distressed (mentally ill) became one, as they came under the flag of principle and commitment. They worked as a team, using their powerful, if not colorful pasts and experience to develop the most undefeated army of all time! How did they do it?

David's army figured out their purpose. For once, each person there knew they were there for a reason. They saw their objective, to put a righteous man in charge of their country, one who was tough, and would rule with compassion and character. Not only Israel's king, but those of the surrounding countries were gaining wealth at the expense of the poor, and using their positions for selfish and sometimes perverted objectives. Those who joined David were in a culture that could not be changed easily. If anyone else became king, disaster would be the result, because only one man in all of Israel proved he would and could rule with God at his side. He had the support of Samuel, the priest. He had a reputation of courage and fierceness, which he would need to successfully lead their military. David had gained their respect.

Even though David was overlooked, labeled as insignificant, and then insane, those old stereotypes couldn't hold back a man called by God. As a matter of fact, his bi-polar (mood swinging) personality, and ingenious (insane) methods were what made him so successful, both in his relationship with God, and as a leader! When he said, "Go," all who followed him did, and they didn't take the time to ask questions, or to look at the guy next to them, to see if he was of another race, or nuts, or from a bad family. No one cared about this, because David had been all of that, and he, the most dysfunctional guy around, was the common denominator. David was a mix of all men, and loved all men. He saw that he was nothing without God, just a mixed up, confused kid. He saw that with God, nothing could stop him!

It's time to see who you are. It's time to get your eyes off of the labels. You've had some "pasted" on you, and if you've ever tried to get a label off of an item you purchased, you know it can leave a sticky mess. But with the eyes of the Spirit, the "oil" of the spirit, your labels, and those of the men and women around you can slide off easily. Labels are only Satan's tools to condemn. We are here to stop him from using any tools.

As we ask God to show us who we really are, and as He does, we also need to quit being ignorant. It's not about us, but about the purpose of putting Jesus on the throne, where He belongs. This world is going in the toilet fast, and now, as we take a stand, all the lies of the gods, and the tricks they've used will fail. All the prejudice will fall away. All the arrogance. All the pride. We don't need them, and the sooner we see we're nothing, nothing at all, the better. We are nothing, <u>until we are in total service to the General</u>! Under His command, we are mighty. Under His authority, we are powerful! And we can walk as one, as long as the one walking beside us is under His command too! That is family! And that, my friend, is the one army that will never be defeated!

I have to say this. Please don't be offended, because it's deep in my soul, planted there by the God of creation. Get up! For God's sake, yes, **for God's sake**, get up and move out! Throw away everything Satan offered you! Run from relationships that don't bow to God! Rush to the side of the General, the one you can trust! Sure, there'll be some changes, but hey, isn't that what you want? Do you have to define it and control it, or can you just trust Him to make those changes, while you simply follow orders? If you can't trust Him that much, then you really don't trust Him at all! And by all means, rebel. Rebel against every negative word spoken about you, every label stuck to you, and every cutting, critical thought you've had about yourself! Do that "180" and never, ever look back. It's time. Now. Not tomorrow. Get up, Giants!

Chapter Twenty

No More Lies
- Early Intervention -

*"How long will your iniquitous and grossly
offensive thoughts lodge within you?"*
Jeremiah 4: 14 (AMP)

We have one thing to conquer and one alone. It is a lie. It looks so small, yet it silently holds us in its grasp. We refuse to move, refuse to act, and refuse to see anything any differently because, in all honesty, we don't believe we can.

But the silent lies will be overcome by the audible cry of a liberated prisoner. A popular prison Bible bears the truth, for it is entitled, "Free on the Inside." But for some reason, we read it but never got it. Not only does it tell us of our inner freedom, it speaks the truth about our might, our unique abilities, and of the one thing we never knew we had; purpose.

First, we must recognize the gods. We must treat them as alive, existing forces with an agenda to kill us. Their voices have to be marked and their influence eradicated. Their worn out tactics must be overthrown.

Second, we have to refute them, and expose them. This will take complete conviction that we are correct, and that can only come from knowing scripture. This means we have to study it, dream about it, and use it, for no weapon is of any use unless the one who possesses it learns how to handle it.

Third, we have to tell. No more prison ignorance, no more fear to take sides or proclaim opinions. No more listening to self-proclaimed "leaders," who are merely wolves in sheep's clothing, or even worse, sometimes "lambs" in sheep's clothing. (That's when a baby Christian with a big mouth let's his ego rule him. He gathers everyone around him, promising to take over the world, but he's still walking around in his own dirty diapers!) We, refusing to stay where we've been, must move forward aggressively. We must also take risks, whenever God asks, but refuse to take the credit!

We willingly go public, but never, ever ask to be in that position. We resolve to answer truthfully, or not at all. We have to permit ourselves to lay down everything, our lives if need be, to attain our calling. Like David, our reputation must be strong, in order to step into our rightful positions.

Finally, but through each and every one of the other steps, we take our thoughts captive to the obedience of the General. Jesus, the Captain of the Hosts, gets to dominate our thoughts. If we're believed to be insane, so be it. All the normal thought patterns, the usual desires and former lists of hurts and hates have to go. We need to make room for truth, for this is the way that we avoid all the old patterns and routines. It's called "early intervention," and is the method we use to stop the battles before they start. And before we open our mouths, we need to find and cling to truth.

When we surrender our minds, we grab the reins of perverted, murderous and terrorized thinking. We "let go" of old ideas, and instead, "steer" them away. Intentionally. We fill our minds with God's Word, and the result is that we begin to recognize everything that opposes it. Not that we have to make all the changes, because that's a rabbit trail too. But we find our role, and stick to it.

And we need to embrace the Giants. This means our thoughts have to contain truth about them too. We have to ignore what our eyes see, ears hear and noses smell. We have to put aside what we've heard and been taught. We have to listen to truth, and run every human through that "filter." Disrespecting them means we risk offending God, for He has called the Giants, and the one we see as odd, weak or insignificant might be one of them. We will risk anything for God, but nothing that could turn against Him. Yet, if we perceive that someone is following the gods of incarceration, Anger, Lust and Fear, we will guard our souls from joining them.

We are Giants. We have been paralyzed monsters, and what little we did for God's kingdom quickly unraveled each time we fell to the gods. Not knowing who we were, not seeing the pride of our Father and the calling He prepared us for, we fell. Now we have to make up for lost time. Without a moment to lose, we must cling to Him and His ways. We can't count on anyone else to do what He's asked us to do.

When we are confronted we must know we are His blood, for every demon in hell will try to convince us otherwise. Every thought we have must agree with God, or it will become a bad seed in the soil of our hearts. We have a job to do, and we must jerk ourselves out of the slumber of addiction and hopelessness, for we are not only His greatest army, but perhaps His last. What we do, and how quickly we respond could well determine what we see in eternity, and <u>who</u> we see there. I, for one, don't want to arrive at His throne alone. I want you there, and every person He loves, whether I have learned to love them or not. My position is not to choose, but to call. He chooses.

Chapter Twenty-One

PEACE IN THE STORM

"Oh Lord, do not Your eyes look on the truth?
Jeremiah 5: 3 (AMP)

You have only One Being you can count on always. In Hebrews, He says He will "...never leave you or forsake you." This is Jesus Christ, part of the Holy Trinity of God. He is a rock you can stand on, and a fortress you can run to. He always believes in you, and loves you beyond life.

I have experienced Him in places of deep turmoil. Through the most painful moments of my life, I have learned to return quickly to my Advisor, my Daddy, my trusted Friend. No one can dissuade me, and I love no one enough for them to pull me away from Him. Even my husband and children are clear on this. In my first marriage, it was the undoing of it, for my passion for God was perceived as competition. It was only in hanging on to truth that I was able to pass that test, and God has richly rewarded me.

I have been promised fame. I have been offered money. I have been threatened, and accused. But I fear only that I could not feel His presence. Nothing else grips me or draws me. The longer I am with Him, the more I want to stay. I daily grow less interested in the things, positions and gratification the world offers me, although I am surrounded with blessings everyday. He surrounds me with them, for as I pursue Him, He seems unable to resist spoiling me. Yet it is He that I follow, not the things He adds to my life.

In the face of human suffering, I am weakened with the desire to offer Jesus. When the opportunity is not there, and I must simply be a witness to earth's depravity, I mourn. When I am able to present my Lord, and when I'm given a chance to share the mystery of His love, I experience fulfillment that compares to none other. This is my peace.

Once, when I was assaulted by someone who was in a great position of trust in my life, I thought I would drown in sorrows. Like an innocent child, I had no protection, and it threatened to crush me. Yet, I had developed such a lifestyle of devotion to God that healing began in an instant. God had allowed a "storm," a life altering, unexpected attack on my life, and He had done so because He trusted me. This I knew, even as it occurred, and my Jesus was the first thing to enter my thoughts, as I searched for a reason. The details weren't important to me, just what my God wanted as a response.

God gave me strength through that ordeal, and He surrounded me with Christian friends. Even though many of them didn't understand it all, they carried me to Jesus in their prayers and words of encouragement. Some rushed to my defense. Others hugged me, and wiped my tears. A few shared dreams and visions, and listened to mine. As I sorted through the mess, God gave me courage to put a stop to the evil. He gave me a voice to end the opportunity for it to ever happen again. A door closed, and I would be the last of God's children to ever feel the pain inflicted by one who called himself a follower of Christ. I was honored to have the opportunity. God's great heart had grieved over the victims of someone who pretended to represent Him. I was thankful to be a tool, to end the masquerade once and for all. No longer in ministry, no longer serving in a Christian organization, this man will not be able to misrepresent Jesus again. I was thankful because that was what had hurt the most.

My peace is in my purpose. I am not here for me, but for my Master. I serve no one and nothing else. I bend to all God places in my life, but bow to only Him. If it brings Him glory, I am content. I know now that the things I've endured were always to show me I could not rely on myself. Even Paul said that (II Cor 1: 9) and I suppose both of us could agree that we are better off passing through trials, than avoiding them.

When I am hated, abused or neglected, I must realize that people hate what they do not understand. They overlook what they cannot see, and abuse what they perceive to be surpassing them. It's easy to take pain when I know I am standing for truth. It's even a privilege to see the darkness I've been in, and the lies I've been told, when I understand that it was because the realms of evil saw me as a threat! Jesus said that we should expect to be hated, as His followers, that they "hated" Him "first." It's really not us they hate; it's Jesus!

We need to represent Him all the more, so that when they seek His love, they'll know that we're the ones to ask.

Peace in the storm is not in the absence of turmoil, but in the presence of purpose. We willingly suffer, when it is for something we believe in. We gladly take the blows, when we are convinced that it's because we are trusted servants of the Most High. We, knowing who we are, that we are Giants who must stand, not back down, not give up, but push forward with tenacity and courage. We can enjoy "rest" later, for we are promised a rest that will never end. Rest is not peace. Purpose that is borne out of the truth of God's Word is our peace. His presence in our lives is enough reward to leave us eternally in debt. His joy gives us strength, and His laughter heals our wounds. We are His dwelling place (II Cor 6: 16) His property.

We are His favorite tool, like a Swiss army knife that He can use for just about anything. Like any great tool, we might look a bit worn, but everyone knows how carefully you guard your best tool or weapon! That's the one that gets the special place on the shelf, and no one gets permission to mess with it! Our peace comes in knowing that, the more we allow Him to use us, the more carefully He will guard us. He longs to show Himself faithful and strong "in the behalf of them whose heart is perfect toward Him." (II Chron 16: 9) It is as we sell out to God, abandoning every other goal or ambition, we find ourselves safe, valued and content. When we no longer want anything but Him, it is then that we are home.

MY STORY

---

*"Even though I (must) walk through the valley of
death and darkness, I am willing to go,
as long as You are with me."*
Psalm 23 (Mine)

I realize that for most of my life, even the years I've loved and served Jesus, I've been clueless. It's quite possible that I'm only starting to understand what this is all about. It's not about me.

I'm not sure when Satan got thrown out of heaven. I know he was an angel of worship, and that he got caught up in his desire to rule, rather than to please the Lord, and honor God as the Ruler. But I do know Jesus called him the ruler of this world. Too bad, because he could have stayed in God's presence. Now he's been given exactly what he wanted; dominion. That's why it's important to watch what we desire and pray for. Usually, whatever we seek, we will find. If we seek God, though, we won't want anything else.

Whatever the details were, Satan found out that he was in charge of a mess! He started making rules, trying to dominate people through their thoughts. He tried to stay invisible, so people would blame themselves and each other for the darkness and evil they encountered. I only recently came to understand that he was behind all of it. In my mind, I believed so many of his lies. Every time I believed, I was in cooperation with his world. I'd been "living" on his "turf," so of course I'd be subject to his rules!

But now I know the difference between lies and truth. When I hear an accusation, whether by a human voice, or demonic suggestion, I refute it. If someone says, "Are you mad at me?" I can quickly respond, "No, Satan's the one that's mad. He just wants to get between us, because he fears our unity."

Satan needs to be exposed. People who admit he's real usually fear him, but Christians have left the realm where he rules. We have nothing to fear, because we're not subject to this place anymore! Even though Satan is the ruler of this world, we are only ambassadors here. We have diplomatic immunity, and can live however we want. We live above every law of vengeance, domination, greed and impurity. We don't have to play by his rules anymore!

As the child of violence, alcoholism, divorce and neglect, I surely was doomed, but as was the case with so many Bible characters, I guess God just saw someone that could never, ever succeed on her own! That was an opportunity for Him, because anything I managed to accomplish would automatically be credited to God; He would get all the glory!

Mom found Jesus, when I was two years old, and that was the beginning of my blessing. I was a retarded child, with mild cerebral palsy. I wasn't extremely aware of the natural world, scientific elements, or concrete ideas. I was in my own world, but one day a Sunday School teacher **bothered** to ask me if I'd like to ask Jesus in my heart! It's my first **clear** memory! That day, the "lights went on," and I began to see deeply into the realm of the supernatural world. It made sense to me, and I have strong recollections of the invisible sensations. I knew God, I knew Satan, and I was very clear on which was which.

Somewhere in the next ten years, through constant criticism and isolation, I had a collision with my flesh. Like the average kid, I wanted, now, to fit in. I began a completely different quest, not to please Jesus, but to be known, liked and admired. Totally naïve as I was, having lived a socially sheltered life, I went about it all wrong. By 15-years old, I was sitting in a girls' prison, a place for serious offenders, too young for state prison, too violent for a juvenile facility. The little girl who'd served Jesus, who'd affectionately gushed over Him in her prayers, and who had generously placed a whole quarter of her dollar allowance in the offering each week, she was gone! In her place was a bitter, violent, selfish low-life who had set out to prove her hatred for God.

Charged with kidnapping, armed robbery, and assault with a deadly weapon, I'd been arrested by the FBI because my crime spree had covered more than one state. The state where I was captured didn't want to deal with me, after I escaped from their facility, took another inmate with me, and managed to elude them for over a year! They sent me back to California, my home state, where I had more charges awaiting me. Here I would wait.

Even though I was so young, the legal system was set on putting me away for as long as they possibly could. They couldn't yet try me as an adult, but they could sentence me to eight years in California Youth Authority, as the system allowed for holding a juvenile until their 25th birthday. This is what the district attorney wanted, and it's what I deserved.

Mom hadn't given up on me yet, and she hired a well-known attorney. I don't even know how much it cost her. The attorney set to work on my case, and the system let me go home to wait for my hearing. Meanwhile, things kept coming up to postpone it. It was really odd, or should I say, really "God."

I attended an evangelistic service where the former president of the Hell's Angels was supposed to speak. He'd given his life to the Lord, and I guess Mom figured I might listen to him. I probably did, but honestly, I didn't hear the words. By the end of the service, I didn't even care what he said. I remember he wasn't much of a speaker, at least to a 15-year old kid. But my heart was pounding so hard I felt like I was going to get sick. I knew it was God, my old friend. For some reason, even though I'd told Him I hated Him over and over, and had set out to prove it, He came back to ask me to trust Him with my life. What a crazy thing to ask a kid who hates You for all the things that went wrong in her life! I mean, trust was the last thing I would have given anybody! But I needed

Him, and I knew He was real. Even in my most rebellious moments, I always knew He was real. I'd never denied it, just decided to show Him how mad I was at Him! I've never understood, to this day, why He wasn't mad at me. I guess He was just waiting for me to see that my anger wasn't making me feel any better. I picture it kind of like when a kid has a temper tantrum, and instead of inter-fering, or getting upset, the parent just leaves the room and says, "Well, let me know when you get done!" I was done. God was there, INSTANTLY!

That night, I returned home. I hadn't wanted prayer, or anyone "helping" me as I cried at the al-tar. I knew Jesus already, and I bonded back to Him with spiritual super glue. I felt like no one could understand how passionately, how fiercely I would serve Him, and that anyone praying for me was a long way from where I was going! The next morn-ing, I determined in my heart that I would never, ever leave Him again. I was pretty sure I'd go away for the full eight years, to a place where kids come out worse than they go in. I thought maybe God wanted me to go in and bring kids to Him. I knew I couldn't run from that, so I told Him, "God, if you send me to CYA, I'll serve you there. I'm never turning on You again, and if someone attacks me for my faith, or even kills me, I don't care. I know You're what I want. Nothing else matters."

I had returned to high school again, and made up the year and a half that I missed in six months. I was attending junior college at night for extra credit, and working in the afternoons and on the weekends. I was getting straight "A's" through all of that, and that was a miracle because drugs had really messed up my ability to concentrate. I compensated for every ounce of the brain cells that had been destroyed with a determination to make up for how I'd hurt God. The six months passed, and finally my hearing came up. I was ready. For anything.

I dressed the way Mom said I should. That was new, but I had no more will of my own. I wanted to bless and please her, because I had nearly killed her. For the year I was on the run, she never heard a word from me; she didn't know if I was dead or alive, part of some satanic cult, or lost in drugs and violence. (In a way, I was <u>all</u> of those things.) For a mom, not knowing is torture, and I'm still ashamed I did that to the woman who loved me so much.

We walked into the courtroom, and it was me, a bailiff (in case I got out of control), a lady from probation, my lawyer, Mom and the judge. The black robes the judge wore reminded me of Satan, and I wondered if he hated me. I deserved to be hated, especially because I'd caused such devastation while "proving" my independence from God! The rampage had included several people being hurt and traumatized, things they probably still suffer over.

Papers rustled in the judges' hands for EVER! I was shaking down to my sandals, and couldn't move. I never looked around the room. I didn't see faces. I stared at the judge, my judge. He would tell me where God had called me.

The man looked up, and the first thing I saw was **CALM**. I didn't expect that, probably because I had already imagined him jumping up and yelling at me. I wasn't afraid to be yelled at; it was just what I figured I had coming. He should have. One of the songs I wrote recently says, "You (Jesus) should have left me to die." Really, in this country, I'm the kind of person the death penalty was created for. But this judge didn't look all that mad. I thought maybe he was cold and calculating instead. He set the papers down, and I wondered if he'd read them all, because there were a bunch! I didn't even know what they said, or if it was all the truth! My lawyer must know, I thought, and I guessed that the judge read some of what my lawyer put in there, to help my case. His voice was really loud, but he wasn't yelling:

"Young lady… (Yada, yada, yada! I faded out again, couldn't concentrate, and couldn't figure out what he was saying. I hated that, 'cause I knew it was probably important. I jerked myself back to awareness, just in time.)…the purpose of California Youth Authority is rehabilitation. From the looks of things, **you're already reha-bilitated**! I'm going to sentence you now to **six months probation**!

The room started spinning, and I didn't respond at all. I just sat there, in total disbelief! Was this the hearing, or was I going to wake up out of some cool dream? More was said, something about the probation officer. She was smiling. That was weird! My mom was smiling. The **bailiff**, Mr., "I'm gonna throw you down on the floor and slap these cuffs on you if you even LOOK like you're gonna do something stupid," **was smiling**! What the heck was going on!

Later, I found out that my good grades, reports from work and the youth leader at church, and the fact that I hadn't broken any laws while out of jail was what had impressed everyone. Hey, my life was on the line! I didn't think that was much evidence that I was such a great person. I thought it just meant I was terrified! But I guess I <u>was</u> different, not in ways these people could see, but in my heart. I didn't want to ever hurt Jesus again. He was my precious friend, and I would have done anything to make up for the pain I'd inflicted.

Two months later, I was released from probation. Not six months. Two months. My probation officer had me over to her house several times, and called me repeatedly over the next year. She said she "needed it," 'cause in her job, she said, she didn't see many success stories. Me, a success story? Chhh! God really did want glory, because any time I was called a success was a miracle! Even though God had healed me, from mental retardation as a little girl, cerebral palsy (I got pretty good at competition sports), I still felt like that little weird kid that people made fun of. I was still gullible, even now, because I didn't have the same ability for abstract thinking that other kids did. God had allowed me to continue to struggle with memory issues, as a little "victory scar" showing that there had been a real mental lack. It was just a reminder, for me and others, that I had been that disabled child once. I actually am proud of those reminders. They help me keep Daddy God in my back pocket at all times!

Now, and for the past thirty years, I serve Jesus through worship. I started playing keyboard as a child, first piano, and then the electronic versions when I joined various worship teams. I became a worship director in 1989, and now work with a worship team called, "the Gathering." We're all pretty much from the same background as the Giants, the ones described in my vision of the Sleeping Giants in the foreword of this book. Brock, the drummer, did time at Pelican Bay. One of the guitar players, Bill (we call him "Bill the Bass") was a major drug addict. Val, one of our backup singers, but also my friend, sister, daughter, prayer partner and hair stylist, came from a seriously dysfunctional background. The rhythm guitar player, Dean, was an alcoholic who, like me, met Jesus at a young age. He didn't have anyone around to TEACH him about Jesus though, which still bugs him because it took him 30 years to find Jesus again. Now he goes to State Prisons, Prison Fire Camps, and County Jail teaching guys about the Lord, and preaching the Word. That's because he doesn't want them to be lost like he was. Most of the guys that help us with the equipment, sound and filling in on instruments have been incarcerated and/or addicted. The drummer I told you about, Brock knows about the "voices" that people want to medicate out of you. He just relies on Jesus, though, now that he's stable in that relationship. He's been running a sober living house for awhile now, and has been a pastor for the past three years too!

Jesus is our Victory. None of us could take credit for any successes or accomplishments. My husband sat incarcerated 11 years ago, in the same jail where he is now the senior chaplain. Jesus brought us together, to make our lives combine into the kind of miracle nobody could deny. I think that's what makes us so successful! He's been a licensed pastor for most of our years together; he got that license two years after he got saved! He preaches, and our worship team ministers at Jesus' feet. Most of the places we go are where we find people like us that went down paths of incarceration, addiction and mental breakdowns.

Our worship team is called, "the Gathering," because Jesus said that wherever two or three of us are **gathered** together in His name, He's there in the middle! We're totally dependent on that, on Him being in the midst of our ministry, because, as He also said, apart from Him we can do nothing. It also says in Zephaniah that God would deal with those who oppressed us, rescue those of us who are lame, and **gather** us; that he would bring us back home.

That's my story, too. Apart from Jesus, well, I'm a mess. I spend every day loading up on His presence, finding out His plans for the day, and watching for Him throughout the day. I'm a 100%, sold out, bonafide, over-the-top, way-crazy Jesus

Freak, because I have to be! I slip every time I even _think_ of doing something on my own. Really! After serving Him for 35 years since rededicating my life to Him, I still fall down EVERY TIME I LET GO! That makes me a cripple, and to tell you the truth, I wouldn't have it any other way. My life, broken and dependent, is His opportunity to do whatever He wants, however He wants.

My husband and I pray for you guys (by "guys," I mean "men _and_ women") constantly. You're what we live for. You're what we're HERE for, and that's become quite obvious. We adore you, and _we know who you really are!_

You can contact us by writing a letter to:

Pastors Mike and Kim Harmon
The Jesus Freak
P.O. Box 53
Mt Solon, Virginia 22843

To order additional copies of

THE THREE GODS
OF INCARCERATION

Visit www.amazon.com

www.ingramcontent.com/pod-product-compliance
Lightning Source LLC
Chambersburg PA
CBHW072130270326

41931CB00010B/1719